Author, age six, guards the gate at his Fletcher Avenue home. 1931

Pasadena Cowboy

Growing Up in Southern California and
Montana
1925 to 1947

John Church

Conover-Patterson Publishers

Dedicated, with love, to my mother and father.
With special thanks to all the friends and relations
who inspired this book.

Pasadena Cowboy
Growing Up in Southern California and Montana 1925-1947
By John Church
Editor, Lisa Smith; Cover Design, Rob Roehrick.

Publisher's Cataloging in Publication

Church, John (John L.)
  Pasadena cowboy : growing up in Southern California and Montana,
1925-1947 / John Church.
    p. cm.
  Includes bibliographical references.
  Preassigned LCCN: 96-85162
  ISBN 0-9653071-2-3

    1. Church, John (John L.)--Childhood and youth. 2. California,
Southern--Bibliography. 3. Montana--Biography. 4. World War,
1939-45-- Personal narratives, American. I. Title.

CT275.C48734A3 1996   979.49'052'092
                                       QBI96-40230

Conover-Patterson Publishers, P.O. Box 5385, Novato, CA 94948

Introduction

Old photographs have always fascinated me. These wondrous images that freeze time and place are like small windows to the past. The styles of dress, scenic backgrounds, inside and outside views of homes and buildings, and earlier modes of transportation are stage settings to be savored and pondered. It's the faces, though, that provide the emotional bridge to what has gone before. A grandfather looks stern and patriarchal in one view, proud and loving in another, and playfully happy in a third. In one scene the face of a parent as a child is sad, bespeaking separation. In another snapshot taken a few years later, that face is transfused by joy and involvement with a loved one. When my face shows up in more recent albums, I have no trouble recalling how I felt at the time. It has been fun and rewarding to link the memories and stories triggered by these old pictures to what journalists, fiction writers, and historians have to say about the times and locales involved.

From the mid-1920s to mid-1940s, Southern California, South Pasadena in particular, was an unusually interesting place in which to grow up. My incubation was also strongly influenced by regular and lengthy visits to south central Montana and by parents widely different from each other. Something of their backgrounds is included here as a prelude and to give dimension to their part in these recollections. The appendix tells about their earlier lives in greater detail.

My mother, Charlotte Phillips Van Cleve, known as Phyllis, was the youngest of six children. Born in 1891, she was raised on a cattle and sheep ranch in Montana. Her parents differed too. Paul Van Cleve, her father, was a quiet, dignified, and gentle man, loved and revered by a wide circle of friends and family. His grandchildren called him Grampy. Mama's mother,

Alice, was an outgoing, determined, and brilliant woman. Granny Van Cleve applied her considerable energy and talents to promoting her area of Montana, running their cattle ranch, and finding wealthy young husbands for her five daughters.

Mama loved to recall her early days at the home ranch. I can imagine how it must have been—six active children of widely different ages with plenty of time and space to pursue their own interests and projects. They developed a strong sense of family, an appreciation of the natural beauty around them. All gained exceptional skills in such outdoor activities as riding, roping, and hunting. Granny brought tutors to the ranch to help her educate Mother and her sisters. Mama's talented and bright sisters also actively took part in her training. She greatly admired her brother Paul who was closest to her in age. The violence and tragic accidents common in the rigorous business of raising livestock made a big impression on her. Like Paul, Mama valued and displayed courage and determination. She and Paul were both quick tempered.

Granny demonstrated her talent in finding sons-in-law when Mother, age 17, was married at the ranch to Thomas Greenleaf Blakeman, a wealthy young artist from New York. The young couple built a large home, Crag Eyrie, on the lower slopes of Porcupine Butte, about a mile from her parents' home ranch.

Tom and Phyllis spent time in Montana, New York, Virginia, and England. They had two children. The oldest, Ledyard, figures in a number of the recollections presented in this book. The death of his younger sister, Leal, at age three was a major tragedy of Mama's life. World War I brought an end to the young couple's frequent trips. Both were overseas in France during and after the war. He served as an air corps pilot and she as a YMCA volunteer. When their marriage came to an end, a few years later, Mother came to Southern California to be near her sister, Agnes. Mama worked for a brief time as a stunt rider in the movies. Soon after, she married my father who had moved to the area a year before she arrived.

My father's background was quite different from my mother's. John Letchworth Church was born in 1884 in Sterling, Illinois. He was the first child of Mary Patterson and Bradford Clifford Church. Eighteen months later, his mother Mary died after childbirth. Papa was left as the only child in the family when his infant sister died shortly thereafter. A few years later, my grandfather married Edith Harden. An active and outgoing woman, she was a loving wife and stepmother. The family moved to Duluth. Except for two years the family spent in Asotin, Washington, my father spent most of his childhood in or near Duluth.

My grandfather developed and managed a large, successful flour mill. He and Edith were able to travel extensively. They took some of the photos of California tourist attractions shown in this book. The family built a summer retreat in nearby Superior, Wisconsin. As my mother did in Montana, my father liked outdoor activities and learned to appreciate the beauty of nature. He developed into a strong, athletic youngster who particularly enjoyed sports such as fishing, swimming, and ice hockey.

My father headed west in 1906, shortly after his graduation from Michigan College of Mines in Houghton, Michigan. He found employment at the Copper Queen Mine in southwestern Montana. This was the first of many short stints at mines and smelters throughout the West during the next few years. In 1907, he was in Nevada as part of the silver and gold rush that had begun at the turn of the century. During the next twelve months Papa lived and worked in several towns that are now ghost towns. He did not strike it rich in the boom but took some wonderful pictures of his surroundings.

He returned to Minnesota in late 1908 and worked the next twelve months with a prospecting survey team on and near the large White Earth

Indian Reservation where he made friends with a number of the Chippewas. When this project ended, Papa left for Montana where he was to remain for the next five years.

My father spent most of his time in Montana in and around White Sulfur Springs, about fifty miles west of Helena, the state capital. John North Ringling, the circus magnate, hired him to survey, plan, and supervise the construction of a railroad to connect White Sulfur Springs with the transcontinental railroad 25 miles south. Soon afterwards he was appointed county engineer and assayer. During this period he became acquainted with the Van Cleves whose home ranch in Sweet Grass County was about sixty miles southeast of White Sulfur Springs. He often received invitations to parties and other gatherings at the Van Cleve's ranch and at Crag Eyrie, the home of Mother and her husband Tom Blakeman.

In 1914 he accepted a job as superintendent of a large mine near Chihuahua, Mexico. It took courage to undertake this assignment, for Mexico was in the midst of a revolution that had begun four years earlier. Pancho Villa and Pascual Orozco, two of the most prominent revolutionary leaders, were from the Chihuahua area where many battles had occurred. At the time my father traveled into Mexico, Villa was military governor of Chihuahua and friendly toward American mining interests. When Villa turned against the US six months later, Papa and other Americans working in the area were forced to leave. Shortly after Papa returned to the US, Villa's troops massacred 18 miners at Santa Isabel in nearby Sonora.

During the balance of 1915, Papa traveled throughout the West and Midwest. He worked the first half of 1916 in the engineering department of the Copper Queen Mine in Bisbee, Arizona, one of the last mining boom towns in the West. He then returned to Helena to work as mining engineer at the Comet Mine. When Papa became convinced that the US would be drawn into World War I, he applied for a reserve commission.

My father considered his time in the military the most important period in his life. Commissioned as captain in the army reserves, he began active duty at Fort Leavenworth, Kansas. He spent six months at Camp Sherman, Chillicothe, Ohio, learning to construct pontoon bridges. In Washington Barracks, DC, he took command of the 466th Engineers, a pontoon train unit. His unit embarked for Europe in August 1918 and spent a month in England before crossing to France. They were in Langres poised to bridge the Rhine when the Armistice was signed. The unit returned to the US and was demobilized at Camp Humphries, Virginia, in January 1919.

Both my parents were inordinately proud of their service-connected activities and passed on to me a strongly positive view of all things related to the military. Many years later, as a grieving adult, I noted that my father had specified that his funeral service include a flag-draped casket. We still display the very same forty-eight star flag outside our home on national holidays.

Papa returned to the Helena area after his demobilization. He resumed mining engineering activities and rejoined his circle of friends in the area. About a year later he moved to California.

The oil business was booming in Southern California when Papa arrived in Los Angeles in 1920. He accepted a job in the geology department of the Associated Oil Company. He lived on Harvard Blvd., bought a car, and enthusiastically embraced the booster culture in which he found himself. Two years later, a friend from his army days, Cy Rubel, who had just joined the Union Oil Company, convinced him that there were greater opportunities there. So Dad began what was to be a thirty year career in the lands and leases department. Finally, in his late thirties, the wandering engineer had settled down.

Meanwhile, Mother had divorced Tom Blakeman and had come to visit her sister Agnes Beinecke and her family in nearby Monrovia. My father, through his friendship with the Van Cleves and Blakemans, had known and admired Phyllis for many years. They got together soon after her arrival. They married about ten months later at the Beinecke home on January 18, 1923.

It's difficult to imagine two more diverse personalities. My father was a quiet, introspective person who liked to analyze and solve problems in a measured and logical manner. Mother was a quick-witted, vivacious, temperamental individual who had led a wide ranging and outgoing life quite unlike most women of her generation. I think each of them envied the traits of the other. Each sought, through marriage, to balance their lives with the qualities of the other. Father gained an exciting and glamorous bride and Mother believed she had found the security and stability her first marriage lacked.

After a short honeymoon near Palm Springs, they rented a bungalow at the corner of Bank and Marengo streets in South Pasadena. They probably chose South Pasadena because it was close to Los Angeles where my father worked and only a few miles from Monrovia and the Beineckes. One of the earliest incorporated cities in Southern California, South Pasadena was a clean, well-kept, middle-class town. It had excellent schools, many beautiful homes, good transportation, and fine views of the mountains. Its name was changed from San Pasqual before the turn of the century. South Pasadena had neither the large number of wealthy inhabitants and mansions nor the impoverished citizens and poor neighborhoods of Pasadena, its larger and more famous neighbor to the north.

I arrived on the scene on December 30, 1924, narrowly missing the New Year's birthday of Grampy and Mother. The newly enlarged family moved into a larger home on Fremont Avenue, near the South Pasadena High School, and the saga of the Pasadena Cowboy began.

Contents

I. Childhood: 1925–1937

II. Youth: 1937–1943

I. Childhood: 1925-1937

Fletcher Avenue scene, circa 1939. Our house is the closest on the left.

Chapter 1 Fletcher Avenue Days

Our Street

I was a disgruntled four-year-old. We had just moved into the big house on Fletcher Avenue. Through the window next to the large mahogany bed in the guest room overlooking the front lawn, I counted the tall, shaggy Washingtonian palms that marched curbside along the patched and uneven asphalt street toward Huntington Drive. The purple-brown San Gabriel Mountains rose steeply behind Pasadena farther north. They seemed very close. I yearned to explore my new street, but I was shut in with a cold.

My glumness vanished when I noticed activity heading my way far up the sidewalk. "Mama! Ree! Come here. Quick!" Ree entered the room carrying a dust mop. Smiling, she asked "What is it, John?" Mama entered a moment later, looking concerned. I pointed out the window. "It's a parade. No, it's a train. Come see. Come see!" As we watched, a marvelous procession of tied-together children's vehicles approached. Several bicycles ridden by older kids towed a line of linked wagons and homemade skateboard coasters. One and sometimes two children occupied each of the "train cars." Most of these passengers appeared to be my age or slightly older. The possibility of being part of such a group excited me. I said to Ree and Mama, "Maybe Papa will help me make one of those coasters. This must be the best street in the world."

Our block lay south of Fletcher's intersection with Huntington Drive, a stop on the Pacific Electric line from Los Angeles to Pasadena and Monrovia. Huntington Drive was the principal east-west thoroughfare in South Pasadena. Its median strip carried four tracks of the PE. During the first quarter of the century its big red cars had brought all of the communities of the area within a short commuting time of each other.

Memory magnifies Fletcher Avenue into a remarkable street. There were famous (at the time) people like Ray Sparling, who assumed heroic stature as a member of the USC football team. There were those destined for fame, like Bill Beedle (later Holden), who was honing his acting skills at the Pasadena Community Playhouse. More important to me were the kids whose personalities, actions, and ideas painted many of the pictures I hold: George Hall, Marilyn Wagner, her brothers Dick and Rob, Bob Aron, his brother Walt, Jim Eccles, Dick Hucks, Helen Bellinger, Esther and Margaret O'Connell, Blanche Marshall, Carolyn Blaine, Dick Beedle, Bob Crouch, the Strangmen brothers, June Rogers, Pete Pfeiffer, and Mason Rothenborg.

We moved to the neighborhood in 1929. I think my father rented the big two-story house at 2011 Fletcher because of the large yard. He enjoyed gardening—raising flowers and fruit. Many of the flowers and fruits common to Southern California grew on our lot. Most evenings my father would get home from his Los Angeles office, change into the bib overalls he favored, and be at work in the flower beds by 5:30. He soon created a botanical showplace with colorful flowers at all seasons of the year. He built a lath greenhouse and grew from seeds many of the plants and flowers that graced our yard.

REE

Marie Gillam (later Keller) had joined our household a couple of years earlier as cook, maid, and housekeeper. She was an exceptional cook, a hard worker, and a strict but loving disciplinarian. She ran the house and me when Mother was away and exerted considerable influence during my early years.

Ree, as most of the family called her, was 19 when she arrived in our lives, recovering from a broken marriage to a young soldier. Raised in Northern California, she had moved to Detroit as a teenager. She returned to the West with her husband when he was transferred to a post in San Francisco. They separated soon after and she came to Southern California to start a new life. In common with most people who accepted domestic jobs at that time, she received a very small salary, plus room and board. She was expected to prepare meals and do housework except on Sundays and Thursday nights. She became in every sense a second mother to me.

Ree was given an upstairs room with bath in the northwest corner of the Fletcher house. Her room opened into the back hall that led past the small room I occupied during my preschool years and to the back stairs. These steps led down to her undisputed domain, the kitchen area. I tagged after her most everywhere she went. I was the only one Ree allowed in the

kitchen when she was preparing food. I believed she was the greatest cook in the world and watched with great interest as she created the wonderful meals I recall from my childhood. My young judgment was validated years later when, on many occasions, she won first place blue ribbons at the California State Fair for her butterscotch pies, raisin-filled cookies, and other delicacies. She let me help with the measuring, mixing, and cutting, and instilled in me the enjoyment I still get from cooking.

My father liked to cook too and usually prepared our Sunday evening supper. He said, "Cooking is just the application of chemistry and common sense." I guess he had plenty of practice cooking for himself during his many years as a bachelor. Mama was pleased to stay out of the kitchen. Although she had a couple of specialties—preparing roasts and making excellent, chewy, chocolate caramels—Mama almost always burned or scalded herself when working around a stove.

When I was about two, Ree left for a few weeks after Mama slapped me because I spilled a glass of juice. After about ten years with our family, she quit to accept a much higher paying job in Beverly Hills as cook and house-keeper for Donald Crisp and his family. Crisp was a prominent English actor who had a distinguished Hollywood career as a character actor in many major films. Ree enjoyed her time with the Crisps and managed to visit us frequently on Fletcher Avenue.

Ree was an active member of the Pythian Sister and Eastern Star lodges. I recall going to the ceremony in Pasadena when she was installed as Grand Matron. She recruited Mama as soloist. I watched proudly as my mother marched in the processional, singing one of the lodge hymns in a strong alto voice. I know Ree regarded Mama as a second mother; hers had died when she was young. Throughout Mother's later life, Ree was always there for her. I don't believe that Mama was able to appreciate and gain full mea-sure of nurture from Ree's affection because of her set opinions as to how one should regard and treat servants.

Just before World War II, Ree moved to Sacramento and married a childhood friend, Jim Keller. She studied and completed the requirements to become a licensed practical nurse. When Keller went into the service, Ree left nursing and worked as an aircraft mechanic at McClellan Field for the duration. After World War II, she resumed hospital work and lived the rest of her life in Sacramento. I kept in fairly frequent contact with her and con-sidered it a privilege to express my gratitude and feelings about her to those at her funeral in 1991.

MARILYN

Next door was Marilyn Wagner, several years older than I, who adopted me shortly after our arrival. Before I entered kindergarten she was my closest friend and mentor. A serious and purposeful youngster, she had strong opinions about almost everything. As I look back, I realize that during that period I was surrounded by opinionated people of all ages.

Marilyn and her family were wonderful neighbors and our families did a lot of things together. There were trips to the mountains, desert, and beaches. Picnics and outdoor activities were frequent. Mother enjoyed playing pinochle with Mrs. Wagner and Mrs. Murray, our neighbor on the other side. There were times, however, that Marilyn and I disagreed and battled. Quite often this was because I didn't appreciate the wisdom that additional age had bestowed upon her. I recall the exasperation she expressed when I failed to respond favorably to her suggestions or ideas. In turn I sometimes became belligerent when she pressed her ideas too aggressively. One occasion that involved my father comes to mind.

I was upstairs taking a bath when Marilyn entered our living room where my dad was occupying his favorite chair, reading the paper, and smoking his pipe. "Where's John?" she asked. Without looking up, Papa muttered, "Upstairs." Marilyn marched through the room and up the stairs. She rushed into the bathroom to deliver her message. I was embarrassed and angry at being disturbed, so I "corked" her. Corking consists of making a fist with the middle knuckle extended slightly and then striking one's antagonist in the arm with this extended knuckle. Properly executed, as it was on this occasion, it can be quite painful. Marilyn stomped out of the room, down the stairs, past my father, and out the door. She was crying and loudly proclaimed, "I'll never set foot in this house again!" This commotion led my father to put down his *Herald Express* in consternation and

*Marilyn Wagner dressed
for school pageant, 1931*

go over to the Wagners to determine the nature and extent of the damage to our neighborly relationship. When he returned, I received a solemn reprimand about striking others, particularly girls.

During the next five or six years, before the friends and attractions of junior high and high school broadened her horizons, Marilyn and I spent much time together. In the summer when I wasn't in Montana, we filled the time with mutually interesting activities. Before he left for work during the hot months, Papa closed the windows and pulled the shades to keep the house cooler. Marilyn and I often played Monopoly in the semi-darkness of our living room. We peered at the game board in the dim light, developing our own rules as we went along. We debated such matters as how much of the colorful money would be issued, borrowed, and repaid. Each of us had a strong desire to win. Some real battles ensued when one of us felt threatened by bankruptcy. Complaints such as "You didn't count the squares right" or "Those three houses on Illinois Avenue weren't there before I rolled" sometimes led to disagreements that terminated the game.

We did work well together on some projects. The magazines that came to our homes—*The Saturday Evening Post, Woman's Home Companion,* and *Ladies Home Journal*—were full of ads offering free samples for a variety of products. Marilyn and I pooled our resources and went up the street to Pool's Pharmacy where stamps were sold. We bought several dozen penny postcards and returned home to get scissors and paste for the job at hand. Carefully we cut the free sample coupons from ads. We filled them out with our return addresses, pasted them on the back of the one cent postcards, and mailed them to the advertisers.

The results were gratifying. Within a few weeks we were inundated with small packages containing toothpaste, cologne, cosmetics, food and candy samples, self-improvement and religious books, and some items whose use had not been clear to us in the ads. It was this last category that seemed to concern our parents most. When the packages began to arrive it was apparent that Mama disapproved of the whole idea. "I don't think children should clutter up a mail system intended for grown ups," she said. But I think the real reason was that she believed asking for samples was improper behavior for those in what she perceived to be "our station in life."

We had to terminate our free sample program after I opened a box marked Sanitary Napkins at the dinner table. I expected praise for finding an alternative to the table napkins Ree had to wash and iron each week. Mama looked horrified and said sharply, "John, give that to Ree at once. It does not belong here." Her reaction was similar to that she had shown a year earlier when upset by a clubhouse my friend George and I had erected in the living room. The walls and roof of this fine structure consisted of a very large cardboard box, retrieved from behind Pool's, emblazoned with large blue letters that spelled KOTEX. In both instances she responded to my query, "Why, Mama?" by saying, "I'll tell you when you are older." She never did.

ONEONTA

I started school at Oneonta Grammar School, about a mile west of Fletcher Avenue. It took its name from the nearby Oneonta Park station of the Pacific Electric, which I learned recently was named for Oneonta, New York, the birthplace of Henry Huntington, the founder and first president of the PE. His electric rail system, utility services, and general development efforts had a major impact on the area. The name Huntington was applied liberally to cities, streets, and buildings throughout Southern California. He made a special grant to South Pasadena of the several acres of land on which Oneonta Grammar was located.

Although the seven years spent in grammar school seemed like an eternity, I enjoyed Oneonta immensely. Run by a warm and capable principal, Miss Maude Harris, the school provided new and exciting activities and subject matter each year. There was an annual spring pageant. All classes participated, each enacting a theme with appropriate costumes. In the first grade we were cowboys and cowgirls. Our second grade costumes transformed us into small versions of ladies and gentlemen of the Washingtonian period.

Beginning kindergarten was a particularly important occasion in my young life. My father had been emphasizing the virtues of education from the time he thought I could comprehend his presentation. Alphabet drills, numbers, simple math, and explanations of the daily newspapers were grist for his pre-school efforts. Although kindergarten didn't quite live up to his or my expectations in terms of academic content, it surely was enjoyable. I mastered such musical instruments as the triangle, sand blocks, bells, kazoo, and—best of all—a snare drum. From time to time, good behavior led to the honor of artfully striking this wonder of percussion to summon the class from recess.

Several of us in that kindergarten went clear through high school together. Some, like Ralph Wood and Walter (later Beni) Reinhold, remain friends today, decades later. My earliest school memory involves them.

Our first kindergarten semester had been underway for about a week. One morning a young boy was brought into our class area by his mother and older sister. Our teacher, Miss Sutliff, introduced him as Walter Reinhold. We stared at this sturdy boy who was larger than most of us. Walter wore cumbersome metal braces on both legs. These were objects of interest, if not compassion, to his new kinder mates. Soon after his mother and sister departed on his first day, Walter asked Ralph and me if he could play with the large blocks we were arranging into a fort. I told him that

First grade boys in front of Oneonta Grammar School, 1931.
Author below and just left of Uncle Sam.

more blocks were stored under the elevated stage. (The kindergarten room also served as the school auditorium.) When he dragged himself through the small, cupboard-like doors to find the blocks, we barred the doors behind him. His cries led to an earlier-than-we-expected release from his dark prison. Prompt retaliation was of course difficult because of his disability. A year or so later, after his braces were removed, we realized the error of our ways. Walter often crudely displayed his latent physical prowess by besting us in wrestling matches or in the castor bean fights that the playground plantings encouraged.

For the most part, I got along pretty well with the various teachers. Mrs. Bradley, our first grade teacher, was the oldest of the Oneonta teachers. She usually glared at us with a stern and grouchy expression. She spent a lot of time drilling us from big phonics charts that she tapped loudly with a long wooden pointer. Most of us found learning to read so exciting that we accepted her admonitions as part of the process. Miss Kotter and Miss Bonner were good teachers in the second and third grades, but the real jewel of the Oneonta faculty was Mrs. Gaydou, the fourth grade teacher. Her friendly manner and obvious interest in us and the subjects being covered made her an admired and effective teacher. She went out of her way to individualize her material and made each of us feel we had great futures. My belief that I can tackle anything comes partly from time spent in her classroom.

Mrs. Robe, the fifth grade teacher, ran her class differently. She classified the wisecracks and clever asides that I had cultivated and used successfully in other classes as just plain sass. To this day, my relatives and intimates are issued rules relating to the fondling of ears. Such prohibitions stem from Mrs. Robe's habit of seizing one of my somewhat oversized ears to propel me out the door to the arcade area. There she warned me about my behavior and sent me to the principal's office. This happened with such frequency that Miss Harris began using me to answer her telephone, file, or perform other minor office chores. I guess the disciplinary effect was lost because I remember those afternoon chats with Miss Harris with much pleasure.

About this time I felt inspired to write a play to implement that year's class theme—pioneers. The completed script included a scene in which the wagon train travelers sat around a campfire singing and listening to the strains of a harmonica. "Strains" is an apt term to apply to the music that was provided. Unable to find a harmonica player among my classmates, I asked my mother only two days before the performance to teach me how to play the required instrument. We bought one at a nearby music store and, with her natural musical talent (she had taught herself to play the piano by ear), we deciphered the blow-suck technology of the harmonica. I was able to render a recognizable version of *Oh Susanna* in time for the play. I have often regretted not applying the same energy to learning to play another instrument. I guess my appreciation of music stems chiefly from Mother.

THE LONG BEACH EARTHQUAKE

Some memories can be precisely dated. In the late afternoon of March 10, 1933, when Papa returned from work, he helped me get ready to paint a swing–chinning bar apparatus he had built in the space between our garage and the Wagner's. I dipped the brush into the white paint and began the first vertical stroke down one of the 4x4's that supported the horizontal bar. As I moved the brush downward, a roaring, rumbling sound started and the ground began to heave and shake. My brush stroke left a seismographic record of the Long Beach earthquake that for many years reminded us of that evening.

People poured out of their houses as the rumbling and shaking continued. Mrs. Wagner thought her son Dick had caused an explosion. A moment before, she had sent him to light the gas furnace in their basement. All of us watched in amazement as our houses and garages swayed and quivered. Marilyn said later that the scene looked like it was being distorted by heat waves. None of us youngsters had ever experienced a quake before. Parents were busy accounting for the whereabouts and safety of their children.

After the noise and movement stopped, excited groups of neighbors gathered to discuss what had happened. My Aunt Agnes drove up a few minutes later. She had seen people running from buildings. She was eager to find out the reason for the unusual behavior. She joined us for a nervous meal. Then we gathered around the radio to hear the news. The quake was centered about fifteen miles away in the Long Beach area. Most of the deaths, injuries, and damage occurred there and in Compton, Watts, Huntington Park, Huntington Beach, and Santa Ana. As we listened, the aftershocks continued. Aunt Agnes was sitting in our big rocking chair that picked up every slight motion. She was able to give us early warning, saying, "Here comes another," as each temblor occurred. Some of them were quite strong.

I was not sent to bed until quite late and found it difficult to get to sleep. I was grateful and glad to see the next day dawn calm and bright. *The Los Angeles Times* provided the grim statistics of death and destruction. We considered ourselves blessed that our town had been spared the havoc wreaked elsewhere.

The Long Beach quake had a major impact on the building codes of California. Many of the schools and other public and business structures were condemned and rebuilt. That earthquake also had quite an impact on those who experienced it—no other quake I have felt since has equaled its emotional and sensory effect.

INDEPENDENCE DAY

During my childhood Independence Day ranked right up there with Christmas as one of the most important holidays of the year. My father, who considered his military service the high point of his life, loved the war-like noise and excitement. We visited the fireworks stands in Monterey Park (the only town nearby that allowed the sale of fireworks) as soon as they opened in mid-June. Firecrackers were selected with care to include such standbys as black panthers, ladyfingers, and the dreaded cherry bombs. We included night pyrotechnics such as sparklers, Roman candles, fountains, and exotically named cones and other devices for the marathon day being planned. We displayed this inventory with pride and anticipation in the corner of our dining room as we awaited the big day.

It was extremely important to be one of the first to shoot off a firecracker on the Fourth. Alarm clocks were set, punks were made ready for lighting, and clothes were arranged fireman-style to facilitate an early morning start. The first explosion usually occurred around 6:00 a.m. The intensity increased until most dogs were cowering under beds or houses by 7:00. My father displayed a huge American flag across our front porch. In later years the corner of this flag was missing, blown off by an explosion of our carbide cannon. My dad particularly liked to fire this cannon which made a tremendous noise. I think he gained his carbide expertise from his days as mining engineer, when he used the same material for his helmet lamp.

By noon the red and gray debris of firecrackers littered the gutters and sidewalks of our street. The smell of cordite permeated our clothes and the whole neighborhood. We usually had an afternoon picnic in one of the neighbors' yards with lots of food, games, and other activities. In the evening we took out the fireworks and gathered to put on a collective show. Unfortunately, most of the purchased items failed to live up to our expectations. The monstrous fountains portrayed in the posters and illustrations at the fireworks stands usually fizzled to heights of a foot or two. The Roman candles shot a few desultory fireballs ten or fifteen feet. About half the items wouldn't fire at all. Of course the retailers had folded their stands and weren't available on July 5 to return the money spent on such duds. In later years we forsook these home displays for the big fireworks show at the Rose Bowl. Now such community displays seem to be all that remain of the once grand and glorious Fourth.

GEORGE

My friend George Hall and I got to know each other shortly before I began kindergarten. He lived in a small house about ten doors up the street. The Halls had bought this small structure from Mr. Eccles, who lived several doors farther north. It had been an orange grove work building of the Marengo Ranch from which our area was developed. George and I were both the only children in our households, and we both bore the same name as our fathers. Actually, George's name was slightly different from his father's. The Halls had added Elliott as a second middle name. This honored an officer for whom George's father worked at the Security Bank. Mr. Elliott had generously given the Halls $100 upon learning of George's birth. The other middle name George and his father did share was Dewey, which his grandparents had selected to commemorate the admiral who had won a glorious victory at Manila Bay.

A brother-like relationship developed between George and me. We usually went to school together, following a wonderful as-the-crow-flies route. It required climbing fences and crossing a storm drain, railroad tracks, a medium-size plant nursery, and many residential lots. We tried to evade property owners, unfriendly dogs, and others who preferred that school children use the longer and more acceptable sidewalk routes. Fruit, small plants, and other treasures that we assumed were expendable on the route often found their way home with us.

We called the storm drain a sanky, an anglicized version of the Spanish word "sanque" that had been applied to ditches in our area for a couple of centuries. This sanky was a concrete-lined ditch about eight feet across with five- to six-foot vertical walls. It was part of a north-south system of drains that carried periodic winter and spring flood waters from the mountains behind Pasadena. This particular drain bisected South Pasadena and carried the runoff from the San Pasqual arroyo at Raymond Hill on the town's north border. Like the single track spur line of the Southern Pacific that ran nearby, the sanky provided adventurous youngsters a north-south means of avoiding the more commonly used adult routes. Just getting in and out of the sanky required athletic ability, particularly when we were quite young. Like its larger counterparts, the cemented-in Los Angeles and San Gabriel river beds, it was empty and dry much of the year. Since it ran under streets and other surface obstacles, it offered an excellent straight-line route. The drain's tunnels under major thoroughfares such as Alhambra Road and Huntington Drive were long enough and dark enough that you couldn't see through them. They challenged our youthful courage and fortitude.

I was six months older than George, which put me in a different grammar school class. I believed this gave me the maturity to guide and direct my young cohort. George had an easygoing manner in contrast to my somewhat more volatile temperament. Nothing seemed to disturb him for long, not even the occasional anger vented by his friend in the form of bee-bee gun shots or verbal abuse.

George Hall and I display the yucca stalk and beach ball used in an improvised baseball game in the back-yard of 2011 Fletcher Ave. in 1934. The white paint mark of the 1933 earthquake shows on the chinning bar behind us.

On one occasion we found a very large bumble bee. Because it was much larger, fuzzier, and noisier than the other bees we'd seen, we were determined to subdue and domesticate it. George bravely grabbed the wings of the loudly buzzing insect. I suggested we bind the bee with thread for transport to its yet-to-be designated living quarters. I said, "I'll get the thread." George agreed with this plan and said, "I'll hold the bee by its back and wings while you go in for the thread." Upon my return I found that the project had to be discontinued because the bee had departed after stinging George. Because of his relatively young age, George was crying and had decided, without sufficient contemplation, to blame me for his discomfort. Fortunately we resumed our relationship a few hours later.

George's mother was a warm, energetic woman who made their home a wonderful place to visit. Many mornings I came by a little early to meet George for our trip to school and Mrs. Hall greeted me saying, "Well here's Johnny. How about some breakfast?" The fact that I had just eaten a large breakfast at home seldom diminished my enthusiasm for such a second repast. Because of this extra meal and purchases from the Helm's Bakery and Good Humor trucks that visited our street on a regular basis, I became overweight as puberty approached.

THE VACANT LOT

Next door to George's house was the only vacant lot on Fletcher Avenue. It was the site of a marvelous network of small roads for the tiny lead cars and trucks available from the dime stores. Only with the introduction of the freeway system, which years later destroyed the crystalline views of the mountains and blossom-scented atmosphere of my memories, was the complexity and engineering of this miniature road system surpassed.

We played mumblety-peg and marbles there with great intensity. Each spring a long, luxurious grass crop sprang up and gave us ammunition for one of our prime recreational activities, dirt clod fights. The presence of occasional rocks in the clods was usually detected by reduced trajectories, increased velocity, and sometimes fight-terminating injuries. When the long grass turned brown each summer, the lot was burned off. The fire presented special risks to the adjacent homes and usually singed and turned brown the hedge along the Hall's north property line.

The lot became increasingly hazardous to the unwary visitor because of the caves we dug emulating the projects of the pharaohs, DeLessops, and other renowned earth movers. Our caves were more like bunkers. Laboriously, we excavated a hole, usually about five feet deep, four feet wide and six feet long. We covered this hole with planks or old doors, and shoveled the excavated dirt on top. We successfully created in that vacant lot a scene much like the Western Front of World War I.

THE ATNOENO

The sixth grade was the culmination of our grammar school experience. As the most senior students we basked in the adulation and respect shown by the children in lower grades. The sixth grade class theme was the age of chivalry. We made suits of armor, spears, and shields and held jousting tournaments that attracted crowds of young spectators. We also published the Atnoeno, the school paper. I will let you fathom the origin of its name. As editor, I prepared inspirational editorials that my family sometimes labeled hypocritical. In the Thanksgiving issue I admonished our readers not to overeat. That year I became ill, vying with my cousin Harry for quantity of food consumed. In the Christmas editorial I extolled the greater pleasure of giving rather than receiving gifts. My relatives indicated that they had not observed this attitude in my yuletide behavior.

In our mid-year class graduation issue I do find some comments by my classmates that reaffirmed the high regard I had for Oneonta School. From the January 29, 1937, issue, under Farewells:

```
I do not think there is
a better school on the
Pacific Coast than
Oneonta.
Bob Abell

I am leaving Oneonta with
deepest regret. In my
esti-
mation it is the best
school in the whole world.
I have never in my life
gone to a school that has
such good sportsmanship.
Bonnie Lathrop

North or South, East or
West,
Oneonta is the best.
Walter Reinhold
```

```
I wish to thank Oneonta
for all the opportunities
it has given me.
Armand Crump-Bell Ringer

I shall always uphold
the high standards of
Oneonta School.
Ralph Wood


As long as I live I shall
remember Oneonta. I wish
all of the teachers and
Miss Harris happiness
through every year of
teaching.
Masami Yamanaka
```

READING

A report card from Mrs. MacMarten, my sixth-grade teacher, contained good marks for "understanding what is read" and "reads well orally," but gave me the lowest possible marks for "reads good books voluntarily," and "uses the dictionary habitually." She increased the attention this card received at home by writing, "John needs to do more recreational reading." (Not pertinent to the literary focus of this particular memoir is the fact she also continued the low marks of previous teachers for such social adjustment items as "works well with others," " keeps occupied," "gives attention," "respect for law and order," "shows normal control of emotions" and "has a cheerful and cooperative attitude.")

My father and I were perplexed by the comments regarding reading because several years earlier he had begun to bring me books he thought might inspire me to greater success in life. As a child, my father had read a number of books by Horatio Alger, Jr., whose background included Harvard, teaching, journalism, and the ministry. From the experience Alger gained seeking to improve the conditions of street boys in New York, he wrote more than one hundred juvenile fiction books during the last thirty years of the nineteenth century. All lauded the virtues of honesty, clean living, perseverance, loyalty, and hard work. Although millions of these books had been sold around the turn of the century, they were out of print when I was a child. By visiting used book stores, my father was able to buy me Alger books with titles like *Ragged Dick, Luck and Pluck, Tattered Tom, Do and Dare, The Western Boy,* and *Strive and Succeed.*

All of these books had a common theme—a poor but honest boy struggled against tough conditions and conniving, evil villains to succeed in the business world. Usually, toward the end, a stroke of good luck or an heroic act by the young man propelled him into the goal he sought: wealth and comfort.

These books had obviously affected how Papa, and perhaps others like him who had come to California to seek their fortunes, looked at life. I enjoyed the books (which I learned later were considered examples of extremely poor writing) and at that early age fully embraced Alger's concept of success.

Other authors I enjoyed were Edgar Rice Burroughs and Zane Grey, who both lived in Southern California at the time. The Burroughs books influenced our childhood play more than any other source. In our play we frequently evoked the Tarzan book characters we had seen in the Saturday matinee movies. George, other friends, and I climbed trees, imitated animals, and staged dialogues and battles based on Tarzan portrayals by Johnny Weismuller and other stalwarts. There was even a large oak at the corner of Huntington Drive and Marengo Avenue that kids from all over town called the Tarzan Tree. Its broad, springy limbs made for exciting climbing and jungle play. Burroughs's exotic books about Mars and trips to the center of the earth stirred an early interest in science fiction that endures today.

My parents also enjoyed and encouraged me to read Zane Grey's stories like *Riders of the Purple Sage* and *The Rainbow Trail*. Such western novels contributed to my concept of the typical cowboy as a silent, courageous, hero, more demonstrative to his horse than to the heroine, but willing to sacrifice all to overcome evil or dishonesty. Mother also knew Will James, the cowboy artist and author. She took me to meet him when he appeared at a Pasadena bookstore. I still have the copy of his wonderful book *Smoky* that he signed for me that day. These books, along with the many Charlie Russell prints around the house and Mama's large repertoire of cowboy songs, added to my belief that we were true Westerners.

Will James's obvious regard for horses brings to mind how much I also liked the Doctor Dolittle books. I found Lofting's concept that it was possible to communicate with animals enjoyable and heart warming. We always had animals around. I learned to love and treat them well. I still believe pets are more aware of what's being said to them than people generally realize. Perhaps the speaker's touch and tone convey more than the words.

It's too bad I didn't jot these notes down sixty years earlier. Perhaps Mrs. MacMarten might have revised her report card comments.

DEATH AND RELIGION

My first experience with death occurred late one summer afternoon when I was ten. For several months we had enjoyed a badminton set that Papa bought. He used a rolling marker that dispensed white lime to carefully mark out on our backyard lawn the official badminton court boundaries. He coached us on the rules, techniques, and strategies of this royal sport. Before long the shuttlecock was whizzing back and forth over the net stretched between special posts, held in place by guy lines pegged into the lawn. It was lots of fun and on this day some of our neighbors joined in the game. Marilyn's father, Rufe Wagner, joined his son Dick to play doubles against a team made up of Papa and Mr. Murray, our next door neighbor to the north.

Quite a few spectators, including Mrs. Wagner, Mrs. Murray, my mother, and several neighborhood children, lounged around the sides of the court. We encouraged the players and commented on the skill and competitive effort they displayed.

Badminton is a fast and strenuous game. Before long the three men and Dick were sweating and puffing, urged on by their relatives and neighbors. About ten minutes into the game Mr. Murray, a small, bald, wiry man, clutched his chest, gave a choking gasp, and slowly sank to the ground.

His wife, Marie, rushed to him. She dropped to his side and cradled his inert form in her arms. The look of anguish on her face was etched in my memory as she said, "Oh, Jimmy," over and over again.

Someone ran to phone a doctor. Mama took me into the house and sent me upstairs to my room, saying, "It's better not to be around. Mr. Murray has had a heart attack. Please stay there until I call you."

I did as I was told and went to my room. I was frightened and upset by the obvious emotion of all the adults. After a few minutes, my curiosity led me to quietly open the door leading from my room to a balcony area over-looking the back yard. The scene had not changed—Marie Murray was still with her husband, and others were comforting her. As I watched, the doc-tor arrived and knelt to examine Mr. Murray. When the doctor arose, he said something to Mrs. Murray and she turned away, crying. They covered the figure on the ground and shortly thereafter an ambulance came and took the body away.

I was very concerned with the speed and finality of it all. A friendly, energetic, outgoing neighbor who had befriended many of the kids and hosted a number of our Fourth of July neighborhood parties was gone. Since an early age I had said a bedtime prayer that included the worrisome phrase "If I should die before I wake." In spite of many mechanical repeti-tions I had never really comprehended its spiritual message or reminder of mortality. This sudden exposure to death left me afraid and isolated because my parents had never discussed death with me or given me any philosophy to apply to the situation.

About two years later, Grandfather Church—who had been living with us for about five years—was taken to the hospital after suffering a heart attack. Mama told me about it when I got home from school. She said Papa was with his father at the hospital. When we sat down for dinner at six o'clock, we had received no word from my father. A few minutes later Papa entered through the glass doors of the breakfast room where we ate most meals. It was clear from his wet eyes that he had been crying. He told us Grandfather had died late in the afternoon. In one of the rare displays of love or affection I ever remember between them, Mama got up from the table and put her arms around Papa. I was extremely moved and upset by the news and by the effect on both of them. Grandfather had been unfailingly kind and patient with me. He had spent hours telling me about his travels and involving me in his beloved stamp collecting. I loved him and knew I would miss him. I concluded that death was indeed a fearsome and terrible thing.

The funeral was held at the Turner & Stevens mortuary in South Pasadena a few days later. I sat with my folks in a family alcove off the main chapel. This was my first funeral. The organ played and there was the cloying, sweet smell of gardenias and other flowers. As the minister began to speak of my grandfather and what a wonderful person he had been, a wave of uncontrollable sobbing overcame me. My mother took me out to the car where I remained until the ceremony ended.

As a twelve year old I was ashamed of my tears and behavior. I felt I had let down my grandfather and family. Even now, with greater spiritual awareness and equanimity in the presence of death, I wish I had been able to handle that distant farewell to Grandfather with more grace and courage.

Papa never discussed his religious beliefs or mentioned God. In my perusal of his and Grandfather's albums and scrapbooks, I can find no record of church membership or attendance. Mother had been christened an Episcopalian; so, as an infant, I was christened in the St. James Episcopal Church on Fremont Avenue. I still have the silver cup and serving bell given to me then by my godparents. I don't believe Mama ever entered the Episcopal Church again after the christening. Although she insisted on my saying my prayers, she, like Papa, never revealed any spiritual thoughts to me during my boyhood.

My religious education began through the Wagners. They were active members of the Congregational Church on Fletcher Avenue, a few doors south of Huntington Drive. Mr. Wagner sang in the choir and Marilyn and her brothers, Rob and Dick, attended its Sunday School. It was only about a five-minute walk from our house.

I was introduced to the church at age five, when the Wagners asked me to take part in a play being produced as part of a Christmas program. I played the role of the youngest child in a family whose activities illustrated some homily regarding the meaning of Christmas. Apparently I learned and performed my lines well; Mr. Burr, the minister, called on our family shortly thereafter and invited us to attend his services. I don't recall the conversation during his visit, but the upshot was that I was enrolled in the Sunday School that preceded the regular services each week. My father would give me a dime for the offering each Sunday morning as I set out for the short walk to the church with Marilyn and her brothers. It didn't occur to me to question why my parents never attended.

Although the weekly stipend sometimes found its way to the candy counter next door at Pool's Pharmacy instead of to the offering, I enjoyed the content and fellowship of the Sunday School classes. During the ten years or so that I attended, I got a pretty good grounding in the Bible, the life of Jesus, and most of the moral imperatives of the Congregational Church. The older classes also attended the regular service, where I enjoyed the music and rituals but found it difficult to sit through Mr. Burr's rather tedious sermons.

SLEEPING OUT

In the hottest months of the year the usually cool nights in our area gave way on occasion to warm nights that lent themselves to sleeping out-doors. Sometimes I pitched an army surplus pup tent that Papa had acquired. I made elaborate preparations that included assembling and arranging blankets, pillows, candles, snacks, and water for the overnight event. Sometimes I was accompanied by our dog Shadow and occasionally by George or another neighborhood boy.

A particular balmy night in early September is the one I remember best. Marilyn and I had asked to sleep outside. We were allowed to take our sleeping bags to the rear veranda of the Wagner's house where the night air was cool. We had flashlights for reading, and after looking at our

Our dog Shadow and me in front of the World War I pup tent in which we will spend the night.

books for awhile, we talked in low voices. The conversation turned to a discussion of the physical differences between boys and girls. To illustrate, Marilyn opened her pajama top and shined her light on her attractive, budding breasts. I was transfixed and left breathless by this anatomy lesson. I reciprocated by illuminating my yet-to-be-developed genital area. Our sleeping bags were about three feet apart. This stimulating activity might have led to closer inspection but a noise from inside the doors to the veranda prompted us to get back into our bags quickly and feign sleep.

This nocturnal show-and-tell recurred from a greater distance a few nights later. When I looked out of my upstairs bedroom window I was surprised and pleased to see the same lovely area of Marilyn's torso being illuminated in her upstairs window directly opposite. The view from twenty feet was not as stirring as from three feet, but I responded with my own light show. Unfortunately, one of our parents noticed this exchange. There were words of admonition and no more coed sleep outs.

POLITICS

Few things received the attention that politics did in our household. My earliest political memory is watching Papa putting a "REPEAL THE EIGHTEENTH AMENDMENT" sticker on the rear window of his Buick. He explained that he considered drinking to be a personal right that should not be restricted by law. I got an earlier-than-I-could-appreciate explanation of the Constitution and the importance of individual freedom. He was a staunch Republican who on many occasions told me that Teddy Roosevelt was the greatest president the country had ever had.

Mama's political beliefs were similar and reflected the conservative viewpoint of most of the cattle ranchers in her home area of Montana. She had heard her parents and neighbors react to the striking miners around

Butte. My mother often used the term "dirty Bolsheviks" to label strikers, agitators, or others who advocated political causes more liberal than hers. Both of the newspapers read regularly in the house, the *Los Angeles Times* and *Evening Herald-Express,* were strongly conservative.

Although my memories of the Hoover-Roosevelt contest in 1932 are fuzzy, I do recall wearing a Hoover button to school and professing my belief in the superiority of Republicans to my friends Marilyn and George. I have more vivid memories of the 1936 race. There were more and larger campaign buttons. The Alf Landon button I sported was a four-inch-diameter sunflower with the bespectacled Kansan in the center. More important, the situation at home was more heated.

My father's sister Alice, who—along with my Grandfather Church—had come to live with us a few years earlier, had just turned twenty-one and was voting in her first national election. She often became embroiled in three-way arguments with my father and grandfather when she professed support for some of the New Deal programs that were anathema to them. One memorable evening at dinner she stated that she was going to vote for Franklin D. Roosevelt. My father, who despised FDR with a passion I had never seen displayed in any other area of his life, stood up, put his napkin on the table, and declared in a loud voice, "No one who votes for Roosevelt can stay under this roof." Alice left the table in tears. She did move out to live with one of her girlfriends. After the election a reconciliation took place. She returned to stay until her marriage a few years later.

Wendell Willkie's bid to replace FDR in 1940 was much more spirited than Landon's had been. A charismatic lawyer from Elwood, Indiana, Willkie had gone from a small town law practice to become a Wall Street counsel and corporate executive. He had switched from the Democratic party. Through a series of magazine articles and speeches he had stirred a grass-roots effort based on a rousing appeal to cast out the paternalism of the New Deal government. He urged return to the rugged individualism he believed to be the foundation of America's greatness. Willkie Clubs formed throughout the nation and millions like my father joined the crusade. We went to a massive rally one fall evening in the Los Angeles Coliseum. Willkie delivered an impassioned speech in a rasping voice, hoarse from campaigning. The roar of nearly one hundred thousand voices punctuated his talk every few sentences, chanting, "We want Willkie…we want Willkie."

When the returns showed that Roosevelt had been elected to an unprecedented third term, our household mourned. I was particularly disappointed for I had been caught up in the fervor of the campaign. One reason I remember the 1940 presidential race so well is that I still have my collection of Willkie buttons mounted on a battered piece of blue flannel board. It has survived many moves and transfers and resides in the memorabilia that others might describe as garage clutter.

Chapter 2 California Excursions

Both my parents enjoyed getting out to visit places and often took me with them to see many of the wonders of our area. Even as a child I realized how lucky I was to have been born and raised in such an interesting and scenic part of the world.

VISITORS AND SIGHTSEEING

Visitors often occupied the big upstairs guest room in the northeastern corner of the house. Mamma followed the custom of the time and paid extended visits to her friends and relatives in Montana and Virginia. It was not surprising that the climate and other attractions led to reciprocal stays at 2011 Fletcher. The many organizations that proclaimed the glories of Southern California to the worl had done their jobs well.

Mama liked to include me in the local sightseeing excursions she took with our guests. My particular favorite was the Pacific Electric ride to the top of Mount Lowe. Thaddeus S. C. Lowe, a famous pre–Civil War balloonist, engineer, inventor, and entrepreneur, and his partner David J. MacPherson made this exciting trip possible. Together they conceived and financed the construction of this combination of electric trolley line and inclined railway that rapidly carried its passengers high into the mountains behind Pasadena. Completed in 1893, it was one of the prime tourist attractions in Southern California for nearly forty years.

From our house, this superb excursion began with a walk to the corner of Fletcher and Huntington Drive. We then caught one of the Los Angeles-bound Big Red Cars and rode to the Oneonta Park Station about a half mile west. There we would transfer to the Mt. Lowe Special that traveled north on the PE's Pasadena Shortline route up Fair Oaks Avenue. We proudly pointed out many local sights along Fair Oaks, the main north-south street in South Pasadena. On the right at Oak Street was the architecturally beautiful junior high where I later spent three years. A few blocks farther, on the left, we saw the Rialto Theater, one of Southern California's best examples of the Moorish theater style so popular when it was built in 1925. Designed for both vaudeville and movies, it had a full stage and large, decorative interior.

Many Saturday afternoons found me at the Rialto matinee along with several hundred of my eager and excited peers. A major juvenile social event, the program always began with music played on a huge and ornate Wurlitzer organ. A gripping serial followed, sometimes silent and stirringly accompanied by the organist. These cliffhangers were usually set in the West. Each segment began with an often far-fetched resolution of the perilous ending of the week before. Then we watched about ten minutes of dialogue and adventures. We loudly cheered familiar heroes and booed the villains. Each weekly chapter ended with another suspenseful and terrible plight that seemingly doomed our heroes. We then saw one of the numerous Grade B or C movies being ground out by the nearby film industry. In the evening the Rialto ran first-run films. During the twenties and thirties major studios often previewed new films there. The Rialto was designated a national historical building a few years ago. When I saw it recently it looked a bit run down but was still showing current movies.

Getting back to our Mt. Lowe trip, our ride took us on up Fair Oaks through the center of South Pasadena's business district, past the American Legion hall on the left. It was noteworthy then because Marshall Ferdinand

Foch, commander of Allied forces in World War I, had laid its cornerstone in 1921. It was noteworthy to me later as the scene of Boy Scout Courts of Honor where we received promotions and merit badges.

Continuing north on Fair Oaks, our streetcar went up over Raymond Hill into Pasadena, passing the site of the Raymond Hotel, Southern California's most famous hotel during the 1880s and 1890s. This fabulous four hundred-room structure had attracted thousands of tourists to the Pasadena area until fire destroyed it just before the turn of the century. While I was growing up, young couples often drove up the hotel's old roadways after dark to enjoy the sweeping views of the San Gabriel Valley and other pleasures. When I was in high school, I heard classmates paraphrase the words of a popular song of the thirties, saying, "I found my thrill on old Raymond Hill."

In the center of Pasadena our trolley crossed Colorado Boulevard, the parade route for the Tournament of Roses each New Year's Day. A short time later we reached the town of Altadena lying at the foot of the San Gabriel Mountains. From there our trolley ascended through the alluvial foothills past stations with names such as Poppy Fields, which reflected the appearance each spring of expanses of golden poppies, the California state flower. I remember visitors from the East in other seasons expressing surprise at the arid, scrubby slopes, unlike mountains they had visited in their home areas. Passing up through Rubio Canyon we arrived at the trolley's terminus at the base of the funicular railway. We then transferred onto an engineering wonder called The Great Incline. Using the technology of Andrew Halliday, who conceived the San Francisco cable car system, MacPherson had designed a steep, doubled-tracked incline, three-thousand-feet long. We sat facing outward in a bleacher-like car that carried us from the 2,000–foot elevation at Rubio Canyon to 3,200 feet at the top on Echo Mountain. The weight of a similar car simultaneously making a

*Bradford Church, my grandfather, took this picture as he
and his wife rode up The Great Incline on the Mt. Lowe trip in 1899.*

descent on the other tracks provided most of the lift for our car.

At the Echo Mountain station we transferred again. We boarded an open-sided trolley of the Alpine division. With varnished wood seats and trim, these handsome cars carried us up the three and one-half miles of narrow gauge track to the Alpine Tavern at the 5,000 foot level on Mount Lowe. This was a spectacular trip over myriad curves and ascending trestles. The view from the Circular, or Rim of the World, trestle was the most memorable. We could usually see the Pacific Ocean and most of Southern California spread out below us. When weather diminished the view, we told our visitor what became in later years the comedians' chestnut for most vista sites: "On a clear day, you can see Catalina."

As we neared the Alpine Tavern, the climate and vegetation changed. It became cooler as we ascended from the dry scrub slopes into areas of oaks and canyons filled with pines. Having left the semi-tropical atmosphere of South Pasadena only a short time before, our visitors were often amazed to find themselves in snow on those winter days when Mt. Lowe and nearby Mt. Wilson were covered with white. We usually had lunch at the attractive Alpine Tavern and took a walk on the trails before boarding the trolley for the return trip home.

Unfortunately the Mt. Lowe trip closed down in the thirties after a series of disasters. The Alpine Tavern was destroyed by fire. Mudslides caused by periodic cloudbursts severely damaged the trestles and tracks of the railroad and funicular. The depression had reduced the patronage to a level that could not justify further investment by Pacific Electric. I remember climbing around The Great Incline with my friend Art Krause a decade later. Weather and vandals had destroyed all but a few vestiges of this wonderful route I had enjoyed so much as a child.

South Pasadena itself had a couple of attractions to which we took visitors. One was the Cawston Ostrich Farm on the town border near Highland Park. My chief memory is of the large eggs and graceful plumes displayed and sold to sightseers. As I recall, people fed and occasionally rode the ostriches, which were tall, awkward, and sometimes moth-eaten in appearance. It was not my favorite place to visit because my young nostrils found the smell distasteful. It closed down in 1930, after nearly fifty years as a prime tourist attraction.

The ostrich farm was positively aromatic compared to the stench of its nearby neighbor the alligator farm. Adults seemed less susceptible than I to the excremental odor of the pools in which the transplanted Florida reptiles swam. Most of the time they gazed at the visitors from their inert positions on the cement rocks of their habitat. From time to time, one of their keepers would endeavor to wrestle with the lethargic behemoths. More action occurred at feeding time, however, when grunts and thrashing tails indicated signs of life. The alligator farm went out of business a few years after the demise of the ostrich farm.

Two more interesting attractions lay a few miles southeast of us. One was Gay's Lion Farm in El Monte. We would drive out Valley Boulevard to this home of Leo, the famous MGM lion. Charles Gay had established the lion farm in 1919 to raise and train lions for zoos, circuses, and other markets like the movies. I remember Gay, a handsome, muscular, mustached Frenchman who wore a pith helmet, boots, and jodhpurs and spoke with an English accent. He conducted an exciting animal training act, telling the audience about the methods and perils of wild animal training as he put his charges through their paces. I had seen two of his lions, Slats and Numa, in jungle movies and was thrilled with the concept of training wild animals. For several years I kept on my bedroom wall a wonderful photo of him riding a large male lion called Pluto.

Farther east towards Pomona was the famous Kellogg's Arabian Horse Ranch. There Mama's visitors, many of whom shared her knowledge and love of horses, saw some of the world's most magnificent examples of this handsome breed. The Kellogg troop went through a series of maneuvers and dance patterns that rivaled the famous dressage performed by the Lippizaners at the Spanish Riding School in Vienna. Our adult visitors were often enthralled by the performance, but I found it less exciting than Gay's lion act.

Some of our visitors, particularly those from Montana, brought a frontier feeling into the house. They wore cowboy boots, western hats, and shirts. I particularly enjoyed the visits of my Aunt Allie and her son Harry Dugro. Both were breezy and good humored with a fund of stories and jokes, mostly about Montana ranch life. When they were there we often had penny ante poker games. Beginning around age seven or eight, I was sometimes allowed to play. I usually enjoyed the games, but had some difficulty accepting the concept of losing. The poker skills learned then served me well on a number of occasions later in life.

My cousin Harry, who had been a childhood pal of my half brother Ledyard, was about fifteen years older than I. He always paid special attention to me and went out of his way to include me in his activities in Southern California. I remember him taking me to the boardwalk area at Venice Beach and the wonderful fun house on the pier. Under one roof were all sorts of big rotating barrels that we staggered through, walkways that were rippling up and down as we tried to hold our balance, and great high slides that we came down on mats. We groped through mazes with mirrors that distorted our images. Air jets blew up skirts. Most remarkable of all, a small roller coaster undulated around the perimeter of the huge room high above the spinning discs, jouncing platforms, and other fun house paraphernalia.

Harry took me on a far more formidable roller coaster, the great Ocean Park Racer. I would never have dared it alone. I was a rather fearful child, perhaps because Mother conveyed her own apprehensions and frequently cautioned against real or imagined hazards. In spite of a sinking feeling in my stomach when the roller coaster car got to the highest point and dropped precipitously, I was grateful that Harry provided a chance for me to show bravery and courage. I have aspired to these traits for as long as I can recall. I do remember that my father was not too pleased with the idea of my going to Venice at an early age, particularly when we arrived home after the prescribed 6:00 pm dinner time.

TRAVELS WITH PAPA

My father was head of lands and leases for the Union Oil Company. His job required frequent trips to areas of known or expected oil reserves. Each summer when I was young, I accompanied him on some of his auto trips around California, either before or after going to Montana. He sometimes added a vacation day or two to the business trip so we could visit an interesting site or scenic area not on the direct route to his business appointments. Papa and I calculated that before I was twelve we had visited every county in California together.

We both enjoyed our time together on those trips. We'd settle into a regular routine. He would give me the road map and say, "You're the navigator, John." I'm sure he could have reached any of our destinations quite easily without me, but it made me feel important to help in this way. It also anchored my memories to places printed on the maps, which aided my recall many years later.

I was also responsible for refilling his pipe. He had several that we

When Papa and I traveled together, we often stopped to enjoy the scenic beauty of California. Here I am by the family Buick near Lake Tahoe. Circa 1934.

rotated. The pipe's bowl had to be tapped in just the proper manner to dislodge the gummy ash from the previous smoke. Unfortunately, I couldn't dislodge the same material that was accumulating in his lungs. I then cleaned the stem with a pipe cleaner and measured into the bowl the Prince Albert tobacco that he favored. The tobacco had to be tamped down carefully. If it was packed down too compactly, the pipe wouldn't draw easily; if packed too loosely, the tobacco would burn too quickly and make the pipe too hot to hold.

I learned a lot about my home state on these trips, gaining an appreciation not only of the varied and often spectacular scenery but also of the geology and history of the area. Drawing on his training and long experience as a mining engineer in the West, Papa identified the kinds and structures of rocks and pointed out varieties of plant life. I was keenly interested in faults after experiencing the Long Beach earthquake. He called my attention to the massive tilting and dislocation of strata in major fault areas. The most impressive was where the San Andreas fault crossed Highway 99, just before we began our frequent ascents over the ridge route to Bakersfield.

Farther north on that same road was the tortuous and steep Grapevine on which Highway 99 dropped into the south end of the San Joaquin Valley. This stretch is etched in my family memories because William Warren Orcutt, a noted petroleum pioneer, and Papa's friend and boss at Union Oil, suffered a serious injury there. He was driving slowly up the Grapevine, resting his arm on the sill of his car's rolled-down window. Suddenly a descending truck that had lost its brakes careened around a curve and glanced into the side of Mr. Orcutt's vehicle, shearing his left arm off above his elbow. The sudden impact sealed the wound in a way that no serious bleeding occurred, and he required little first aid. Soon thereafter he was able to return to his active life with an empty sleeve to remind all who knew him, including a young boy, of his accident and the dangers of the

Grapevine.

Our more common route north was Highway 101. We entered this major north-south coastal route in Hollywood, followed it over the Cahuenga Pass, turned west across the southern end of the San Fernando Valley, crossed some hills, and emerged on the coast near Oxnard. The drive north along the Pacific provided great views of the Channel Islands and the scenic coastal area from Ventura to north of Santa Barbara at Gaviota. There the road turned inland, passing through a narrow passage between two high rock cliffs. My father told me that Indians had poured hot oil down from these rocks onto enemies to keep them out of their territory. Later, after learning more about the gentle, acorn-eating tribes of California, I doubted the accuracy of this tale.

Our most common destination was Santa Maria where Papa was acquiring leases for the expanding oil fields in the area. It was also his favored overnight stop when driving to San Francisco. We always stayed at the Santa Maria Inn, whose beautiful gardens and warm hospitality were famous in California. The manager and staff knew my father well. We were fussed over and given excellent accommodations and service. Ferdinand Pimentel, the manager, got to know me too and made me feel especially welcome. The huge displays of gladiolas and other cut flowers in the dining and lobby areas came from flower fields around Santa Maria, which at the time supplied most of the florists on the West Coast. These flower growers were also the source of many of the gladiola bulbs and dahlia roots that produced such wonderful flowers in our yard at 2011 Fletcher.

I noticed on the business portions of these trips how Papa's language changed when he was talking to farmers and ranchers with oil under their land. During my childhood, I never heard him swear or tell off-color jokes at home or in the presence of family or friends. But when he discussed crops, water systems, weather, and other matters with these landowners,

Papa sprinkled in many "damns," "hells," and earthy expletives in a manner quite different from his gentle one at home. I guess this personality switch worked; he was successful in leasing land for many of Union Oil's most productive fields.

My exposure to rough "western" language began earlier in Montana where curses and general profanity abound, particularly when dealing with livestock and other challenges of ranch life. Mama and her relatives and friends were not as careful as my father to curb their adjectives and story telling around me in either Montana or Southern California.

Our travels enabled me to become acquainted with San Francisco. I was captivated by the bay, hills, and higher buildings—so different from the center of Los Angeles. Here too, Papa had a favorite place to stay, the Palace Hotel. We ate in the Palm Court, where my dad told me of the Palace's major role in the city's history. He told of how carriages would drive into the palm court area when his father stayed there at the turn of the century. He described how fire had destroyed the hotel after the 1906 earthquake and pointed out the splendor of its reconstruction. Papa recounted many of his visits. He was at the hotel when President Harding died there in 1923, the year before I was born. Sometimes we rode the cable cars or visited Chinatown, the Cliff House, and the Sutro Baths that had the biggest inside swimming area I had ever seen. If we were going on north we took the ferry either to Oakland or Sausalito and, during the mid–1930s, saw the impressive bridges under construction.

Once we took the Delta Queen on the bay-river trip to Sacramento. We drove our car on board the great paddle-wheeled steamboat. Papa and I had a cabin of our own for the overnight trip. It was fun to eat meals aboard in the fancy dining room and talk with the colorful people in the lounge area. Papa whispered to me, "Those slick looking men are river boat gamblers." I learned many years later that the pretty women, whose fancy dresses, heavy makeup, and friendly manner impressed me so, were actively practicing a long established profession. Today the Delta Queen is a popular, but more staid, tourist attraction on the Mississippi.

On the vacation side trips we saw most of the well-known scenic attractions of the state. We visited the national parks, Yosemite, Mt. Lassen, and my father's favorite, Sequoia—King's Canyon. We traveled the Redwood Highway in Northern California and made the magnificent, twisting trip down California Route One as it followed the rugged coastline from Carmel to Morro Bay.

I have vivid memories of traveling north from the Mojave desert through the Red Rock Canyon area, and over dry and arid mountains into the Owens Valley. We motored for miles along the rugged, up-thrust, eastern face of the Sierra Nevadas, a spectacular vertical wall of cliffs, crags, and mountains rising more than two miles above the valley floor. We sometimes stopped in the small town of Lone Pine, a scant few miles from Mount Whitney, then the highest peak in the US.

We traced much of the route of the Los Angeles aqueduct, which brought water to Southern California from the Owens River valley. As a geologist and engineer, my father appreciated the rugged scenery and was particularly interested in its use. He admired those who designed and constructed this massive water project. Many years later, after reading authors such as Stegner, McWilliams, and Starr, I came to realize what a defining part such water reclamation projects played in the development of the West.

From the Owens Valley we continued north past the bleak and strangely shaped shoreline of Mono Lake, up through Bridgeport into the forested areas around Lake Tahoe. On trips such as this, I was always glad to leave the arid desert areas for the green coolness of the mountains.

My interest in the desert and its scenery never matched that of my father. Papa gained great pleasure from visiting the desert areas that were never very far away in Southern California. At least once a year we made day trips out into the desert area around Palm Springs and the northern part of the Imperial Valley. We sometimes brought home specimens of the plants and animals. At Fletcher Avenue I had a small cactus garden made up of items garnered from such trips (and also from the nursery that George and I passed through on the way home from school). Much of the time we had a small horned toad brought from the desert living on a window sill eating flies trapped by the screen. For a number of years, Teddy, a large tortoise, lived in a pen in our back yard. From time to time he emerged from an underground den to munch on lettuce and other proffered vegetables and allow his head to be scratched. Tortoises fall far short of dogs and cats on the affection and fun scale as children's pets. I realized a few decades later that it was cruel to keep him. On the several occasions he escaped, we found him a few blocks away, always trudging slowly east toward the Palm Springs desert where he was born.

Except for pictures showing Papa visiting the Lazy K Bar when I was an infant, he was not with us in Montana. So it was surprising to see him on horseback when on several occasions we visited ranches in the Sierras or in the Trinity Alps area of Northern California. He enjoyed trout fishing and carried a metal telescoping fishing rod with him in the car. The fishing along the main highways was poor and only by getting off the beaten track could he get the kind of trout fishing he recalled from his days in Montana. Several times we visited a resort outside Kernville, on the south branch of the Kern River. To reach it required a three hour horseback ride. The accommodations were comfortable and the fishing good. I believe the dam-created Lake Isabella now covers the resort site.

My father was not a purist when it came to trout fishing. Unlike some of my Montana relatives and many of the fly fishermen who visited the dude ranches in Montana, Papa believed it was more important to catch fish than demonstrate angling skill with a fly. If he couldn't raise a trout with a fly, he would not hesitate to substitute live grasshoppers, worms, or salmon eggs to achieve his purpose. Although I caught trout using his approach as a youngster, for most of my life I have pretty much stuck to flies as my favorite form of trout fishing. Like fly fishermen everywhere, I received validation for this approach from Norman Maclean's *A River Runs Through It*. The wonderful motion picture based on it was filmed in the Livingston, Montana area where I spent so much time as a child.

ACTIVITIES WITH MAMA

Many excursions with Mama did not involve sightseeing and were different from the activities I shared with Papa. She enjoyed our proximity to Hollywood and the entertainment opportunities nearby. She took me to my first movie when I was still a preschooler. Her friend Margaret Tabb was visiting from Virginia and the three of us went into downtown Los Angeles to the show at the Paramount. The theater was one of the largest and most ornate in Southern California. Its program consisted of both a movie and a big vaudeville show.

The movie, an early talking picture, was *Cohen & Kelly in Africa*, which featured two well-known vaudeville stars who, as this picture demonstrated, never made a successful transition into cinema. The plot had them trekking in darkest Africa as inept explorers. The scene I remember best was of a golf game held with minstrel-show-type black cannibals using pygmy skulls as golf balls. Nevertheless, the whole concept of moving pictures and the big images on the screen thrilled me. The vaudeville show was exciting too. It included a big orchestra, comedians, a chorus line, and a troupe of talented moppets called the Meglin Kiddies. They were able to execute what appeared to be fairly difficult and intricate tap dance routines with glittering smiles never leaving their curl-surrounded faces. We made many visits to the Paramount in subsequent years—Cab Calloway's band was great, the movies were better, and the vaudeville acts featured many talented artists, but the Meglin Kiddies' act remained the same.

Mama loved horse racing. It delighted her when the Santa Anita Race Track was built on the Lucky Baldwin property in Arcadia, only a few miles east of our home. The racing season at this beautiful track ran from late December to March. She loved to go the track early in the morning and watch the workouts. She had a special pass to the stable area and had become acquainted with a number of the trainers and stable personnel. Mama even collected hair from the tails of several of the winners of the Santa Anita Handicap. She intended to have a horsehair belt made from these distinguished strands. We also visited the paddock just before each race because she liked to check the appearance of the horses before betting. She picked quite a few winners, but like most patrons her overall pattern was the loss of a few dollars each time she visited the track. This was a source of some annoyance to my father who considered going to the races a waste of time and money.

Her love of horses also took us to polo matches at the nearby Midwick Country Club and to the Riviera Country Club located near the coast in Pacific Palisades. Riviera was at that time connected with the Los Angeles Athletic Club, which my father had joined soon after coming to Southern California. After her marriage to Papa my mother had from time to time gone horseback riding at Riviera and become acquainted with Snowy Baker, the Australian who had taken over the equestrian activities for the LAAC. She particularly liked the celebrity polo matches held at Riviera. Many Sunday afternoons we joined the enthusiastic spectators that watched Will Rogers, Spencer Tracy, and other stars who joined Baker racing up and down the field in this exciting sport. It was quite different from the Montana version of polo played in the big corral at the Lazy K Bar.

Mother's prowess at sharp shooting was evident in some of the other things we did together. The Union Oil Company had an annual turkey shoot we often attended. Unlike the turkey shoots in earlier days, in which live turkeys buried to their necks were shot at from a distance, these meets involved target shooting with rifles. Those with best scores won certificates good for cleaned and dressed turkeys. Mother nearly always won the women's prize. I also recall staying overnight with her at the Pacific Coast Club in Long Beach, one of the LAAC clubs. We visited the shore-side boardwalk in the evening. At a shooting gallery Mama picked up a pistol. I was proud to see her win a ten dollar bill by shooting all the spots out of a playing card at a distance of about ten feet.

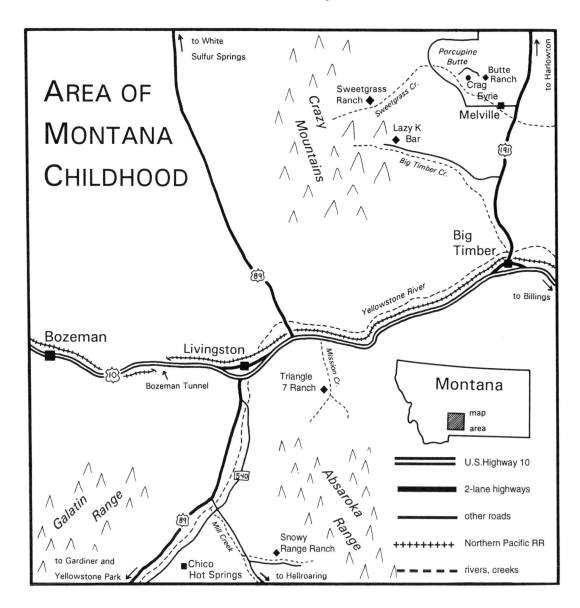

AREA OF
MONTANA
CHILDHOOD

to White
Sulfur Springs

to Harlowton

Porcupine Butte

Butte Ranch

Sweetgrass Ranch ◆

Sweetgrass Cr.

Crag Eyrie

Melville

Lazy K Bar ◆

Big Timber Cr.

191

Big Timber

Yellowstone River

to Billings

Bozeman

Livingston

Triangle 7 Ranch ◆

Mission Cr.

89

10

Bozeman Tunnel

Montana

map area

540

Galatin Range

Absaroka Range

Snowy Range Ranch ◆

89

Mill Creek

to Gardiner and
Yellowstone Park

Chico Hot Springs

to Hellroaring

═══	U.S. Highway 10
▬▬▬	2-lane highways
───	other roads
+++++++	Northern Pacific RR
─ ─ ─	rivers, creeks

Chapter 3 Childhood in Montana

SOUTH CENTRAL MONTANA

The Yellowstone River defines the area of my Montana experience—all the ranches and towns where I spent time were on it, or on rivers and creeks that flow into it. Its source is in the national park, which also derived its name from the distinctive yellow rock formations of the deep and spectacular canyon the river carved there on its way north to Montana. The Yellowstone figures prominently in my parents' history and my childhood days. In 1806, William Clark of the Lewis and Clark Expedition traveled over five hundred miles by boat down the Yellowstone as he returned from the epic journey to the Pacific. Seventy years later my grandfather Paul Van Cleve came west to work for the Northern Pacific that followed the river's path to Livingston as it pushed its new transcontinental lines across Montana.

My opportunity to get to know this beautiful part of the world came about from Mama's annual practice of "going home" to Montana for about three months each summer. For my first six or seven years, Ree and I accompanied Mama or traveled together to join her for the major part of these yearly visits. The idea that home to Mama was not in Southern California and that she took these extended absences reflected a less than close relationship between my parents. I never heard Papa complain of her annual departure. As I recall, he seemed happier when she was away.

TRAIN RIDE TO MONTANA

An important part of my Montana experience was the train ride back and forth. Except when I was very young, Mother's stay was longer than mine, so I usually traveled with Ree. When I was nine, I began making the trip by myself, which was very exciting.

After supper on the day of my departure, Papa would drive me to the East Los Angeles Union Pacific Train Station, about five miles south of our home. When we got to the Spanish-style depot, we looked up my Pullman Car number in the sheaf of long tickets the railroads issued for such trips. We then carefully positioned ourselves to be at the proper spot to board the train that had left Los Angeles fifteen minutes earlier. When the train arrived Papa had a quick word with the porter and gave me a farewell hug. I clambered aboard and waved good-bye from the vestibule as the train pulled slowly out of the station.

The porter and I entered the sleeping car and went down a narrow aisle by the windows past the rest rooms and compartments. When we came to the main part of the car I found the berths made up for the night. Heavy green curtains covered the upper and lower sleeping berths on each side. I was pleased to find I had a lower, so I would be able to look out the window. The conductor showed up soon after to collect my ticket and tell me about the transfer I would have to make in Salt Lake City.

It was wonderful to lie in the comfortable bed, my toilet kit and clothes stowed in the little green mesh hammock that hung across the end, and watch the lights and trackside sights of Southern California towns glide by. Since I fell asleep with the shade up, the early morning sun awakened me the next morning somewhere in the desert northeast of Las Vegas.

During my annual trips with Mama or Ree I had learned the routine of the train. I made my way to the men's room. The porter was often there.

These black men were unfailingly kind and helpful. They made a special effort to make sure that I was doing all right. I followed the admonition on the posted sign: "Please Complete Your Toilet Quietly and Quickly for the Benefit of Other Passengers."

Previous train trips had taught me that completing your toilet included things like brushing your teeth and combing your hair as well as using the toilet. Always one to focus on the details of sanitation, I thought it not quite right that the toilet flushed right onto the trackside area, with a quick view of the rushing ground and a sudden amplification of the clickity-clacking noise of the wheels.

On the swaying walk to the dining car, I used my shoulder to push open the heavy doors at each end of the cars. Glimpses of the moving track bed between the cars caused some trepidation. I imagined and wondered how it would be to make such a passage on a freight train. The dining car on the train was impressive—white tableclothes, heavy silverware, vases of flowers, white-jacketed waiters, and a steward who seated you. I was proud to be traveling alone and pleased to tell the people with whom I shared the table about my destination. I talked with what I supposed was adult perspective about life in Montana and Southern California.

It was usually very hot during the daylight hours. The Union Pacific route from Los Angeles to Salt Lake crossed the high desert. Pullman cars were one of the earliest users of air conditioning. Every few hours the train stopped to take on water for the steam locomotive and to load the blocks of ice that were stowed in the ventilation system of each sleeping car.

My favorite car was the last one on the train, the observation car. This was a luxurious parlor car with a small galley for preparing light refreshments and a few sleeping compartments. Most important, from my standpoint, was the observation platform at the rear. This was a five by ten foot area, covered by an overhanging roof. Railings enclosed the three rear sides. Chairs were provided for passengers who wished to sit outside. In spite of the heat and cinders from the steam engine, I would spend many hours, usually by myself, watching the tracks recede and enjoying the Utah desert sights.

At periodic stops in towns such as Modena, Lund, Oasis, and Lynndyl passengers could get out and stretch their legs. Indian vendors met the train to sell blankets and jewelry. My preference was to buy one of the rapidly melting ice cream cones carried in special cardboard trays by other vendors. It was like being in an oven as we watched the fireman direct the big spout from the track-side water tower into the locomotive. Heat waves distorted distant buildings and trees. It seemed downright cold when we reentered the Pullman cars.

Sometime in the middle of the afternoon we reached Salt Lake City. A Travelers Aide representative met me to make certain that I handled the transfer to my Montana train. When there was time I walked into the center of Salt Lake City. I always found this bright, clean city with its imposing Morman church buildings and mountain back-drop very impressive. If I had time to kill, I would usually hang around the lobby of the Hotel Utah where I had been with Mother or Ree on previous trips. I had to be back at the station in the early evening to catch the overnight train to Butte or West Yellowstone. Another overnight Pullman trip took us up through Ogden and Pocatello over what used to be called the Oregon Shortline route of the Union Pacific. At Pocatello the train split into two sections: one going to West Yellowstone and the other headed for Butte.

Although it was fun to be picked up in West Yellowstone and driven by auto through the park to Montana, I preferred going through Butte where I transferred the next morning to the Northern Pacific. Butte was a big, dirty mining town. Thirty years earlier, Papa worked in several mines and smelters near Butte. During my trips it was gradually losing its grip on the title: Copper Capital of the World.

I boarded the Northern Limited for the four or five hour trip to Livingston. This was the classiest train I ever rode; it had mahogany woodwork, brass light fixtures, and beautifully appointed dining and observation cars. I was usually pretty grubby from my previous day's observation-car ride. That didn't deter me from enjoying the splendor of the Northern Pacific dining car and the special treat of one the immense Idaho baked potatoes that were their specialty.

The train passed through the beautiful area where the Jefferson, Madison, and Gallatin rivers join to form the source of the Missouri River. Pulled by what were at that time the largest and most powerful steam locomotives in the world, we climbed toward the high point of the trip. This was the fearsome Bozeman Tunnel, then one of the longest railroad tunnels in North America. I remember sitting out on the observation car platform and pretending to others that I didn't know the six-mile long tunnel was coming. Passengers who had traveled the route before would come out and try to explain to me what was about to occur. My performance ended when the conductor told me to go inside.

As the train slowly entered the railroad yards at Livingston, I saw the immense four-wheel-drive Baldwin locomotives waiting on sidings to pull the next westbound train over the Bozeman grade. I always felt good about having made the trip by myself.

THE LIVINGSTON ROUNDUP

Often my trip to Montana was timed to bring me into Livingston at the start of one of the nation's premier rodeos, the Livingston Roundup, held for three or four days around July Fourth. When the train came to a halt at the station, which was bedecked with red, white, and blue bunting, Mama, Aunt Allie, and Harry were there to meet me. Harry grabbed my bags and we walked over to the Murray Hotel, their favorite hangout during the festivities. Many of the rodeo riders stayed there. From their spot in the busy lobby Mama and Aunt Allie could see all their relatives and friends who were in town for the biggest summer event in Montana. There was always a big parade through town. Sometimes we rode in it. To see so many real cowboys in one place thrilled me.

Many relatives, Uncle Paul and several of my Van Cleve and Langston cousins, were in the rodeo held in the big grounds south of town. Bronc and bull riding, bulldogging, calf roping, and the antics of the brave clowns who diverted the attention of the angry bulls from fallen riders all contributed to a spectacular show. The town was a wild place with much carousing, drinking, and fighting. Sometimes I was allowed to briefly attend the dances in the night club located on an island in the Yellowstone River. As I watched the noisy revelry and western dancing, I stored up the wild sights and sounds for the stories I would tell my friends back in South Pasadena.

Lazy K Bar

During my earliest years in Montana, we stayed at various ranches owned by relatives in Sweet Grass and Park counties. We spent more time at the Lazy K Bar than at any of the others. Uncle Paul had recently acquired the Bernie Mjelde ranch in the Crazy Mountains' rugged Big Timber Canyon. In 1922, he and Aunt Helen began to build a guest ranch there. Their goal was to attract well-to-do east coast families who enjoyed horseback riding, the outdoors, and the opportunity to experience the activities of a working cattle ranch. The Lazy K Bar was one of the first dude ranches in Montana and became one of the best known in the US. Financing was provided through loans from relatives and acquaintances. Some of the ranch's expansion was helped by a few of the early guests (dudes) who paid to have cabins built; they could use the cabins when they chose, but the titles stayed with the Van Cleves.

Paul and Helen did a great job of developing the Lazy K Bar and managed it during the period covered by these recollections. They took a page from his mother's book and traveled east every winter to promote the ranch and enlarge the circle of people who visited it each summer. Over the years it has enjoyed a reputation for beautiful scenery, excellent riding, and high quality accommodations and service.

My half brother Ledyard, Aunt Allie, and her son Harry were usually there when Mama, Ree, and I were. As teenagers, Ledge and Harry helped with the wrangling and other chores. The lodge and first guest cabins were built in a relatively level area in this rugged canyon, about a hundred feet above Big Timber Creek. The saddle sheds and corrals were down near the creek. We stayed in a cabin near the corrals. A screened cage was built near the cabin's entrance to provide outside confinement and fly protection for me during my toddling years. I have little recall of those first few summers at the K Bar. However, my son John and I happened to be at the ranch when it celebrated its fiftieth anniversary. We saw home movies shot during the first years of the ranch's operation. These films included pictures of all of us who were there at the time.

Paul and Helen's son Spike and his wife Barbara took over the management of the dude ranch in the 1970s. Aunt Helen and Uncle Paul continued to be involved in ranch operations until their deaths a few years later. Spike wrote two books that wonderfully evoke ranch life in the Melville area of Sweet Grass County during this period. Both were published by

Lowell Press: *40 Years' of Gatherin's* (1977) and *A Day Late and a Dollar Short*, published after Spike's death in 1982.

When I was still quite young, about three or four, we also spent parts of the summer at the Triangle Seven about eight miles east-southeast of Livingston on Little Mission Creek. The ranch had been purchased about five years before by Tom Burgess, who married my cousin Theo Beinecke.

Photos from Ree's albums show that she and Theo considered themselves representatives of the Flapper Era. When the Triangle Seven was deserted, these young women enjoyed posing for glamour snapshots, artfully draped with scarves or small furs. When I was older, about eleven or twelve, I found some of these semi-nude shots in Ree's boxes, which she had stored in my lean-to clubhouse at Fletcher Avenue. When I showed George Hall and Walter Reinhold one distant shot of Ree unclothed in front of an unfinished log cabin, they echoed my interest and delight.

SNOWY RANGE RANCH

As I grew older, summer visits to Montana became more interesting. I began to take a more active part in ranch activities. Starting when I was about five we spent most of the next five summers at the Snowy Range Ranch. It was on the East Fork of Mill Creek about twenty-five miles south of Livingston. My cousin Harry Dugro had bought the beautiful property in the Absarokas Range and registered its new brand the HD Bar. He and his mother, my Aunt Allie, along with Kester Counts, began the big job of developing it into a dude ranch patterned after the Lazy K Bar. Kester Counts, whose relationship to Aunt Allie was unclear to me, was a drawling, articulate mountaineer from the Appalachian area of Virginia.

Ree in front of a log cabin under construction at Triangle Seven Ranch. Circa 1928.

Mama and I pause while fording Mill Creek at the Snowy Range Ranch.
I am riding Prunes in this 1930 photograph.

Mama considered Counts a red-necked hillbilly and unsuitable as a companion for her Van Cleve sister, but he made quite an impression on me. An avowed socialist and supporter of Norman Thomas, Counts displayed a vast fund of economic and political knowledge. He had strong opinions, diametrically opposed to those of my parents. His knowledge of nature and geology in particular seemed wondrous to me. His nephew Clyde also lived and worked at the ranch. Mother often made deprecatory remarks and asides about Kester and "Cousin Snide," but her political debates with Counts usually ended in her angry retreat in the face of his more logically marshaled arguments.

The first horse I remember riding by myself was Prunes at the Snowy Range. Mama believed that young children should not use saddles. I think this was chiefly due to her excessive concern about possible injury from stirrup hang-ups. In any case, she always insisted that bareback was the best way to learn to ride. Over thirty years old, Prunes was swaybacked. This provided a saddle-like area which, along with a handful of mane, made a secure seat for me as we trudged around the ranch and nearby trails. I needed to find a tree stump or hand-up to get on him, but I was very proud to be up so high and reveled in the cowboy feel of it all. I was incredulous when Harry and Kester told me that Prunes had been on the stage in his earlier years. My Southern California upbringing made me think they were saying Prunes had appeared in vaudeville. They meant he had served as part of a stagecoach team between two Montana towns.

The ranch was in a timbered valley with rugged peaks all around. A clear, swift stream flowed through. I learned to fish in this creek and listened with awe to Kester's accounts of his exploration of the Crystal Caves that lay by trail five miles up the valley. Mother was horrified when she heard his descriptions of squeezing on his stomach through confined pas-

*My Aunt Allie Durgro,
a virtuoso of wood stove
cooking, poses by a Montana
cattle drive chuck wagon.
Circa 1925.*

sageways that flooded out at certain times of the year. He brought back crystals found in the caves and stories of cavernous rooms, underground rivers, and waterfalls. I was never allowed to make the trip to the caves. I felt this unfair because Mama had told me of her visits as a young woman to the cave at Mammoth Hot Springs in Yellowstone Park. There they had to go down a vertical vent over one hundred feet by rope ladder to reach the caverns below.

The rocky terrain on the way into the Snowy Range Ranch made building an adequate entry road very difficult. A great deal of dynamite blasting was required. I often accompanied Kester, Harry, and Clyde when they were doing this rock and stump removal. It was like an expanded Fourth of July to duck down behind big boulders and hear the boom of the explosion and the rattling rain of rocks and debris showering down. When Mama was around she often curtailed my participation in blasting and tree felling. I sometimes rode Prunes as he dragged logs to the sites of the new cabins under construction. As I got older I helped by bringing water, nails, and other supplies to the men as they finished the roofs and interiors of the cabins.

Aunt Allie contributed a lot to the fond memories I hold of the Snowy Range ranch. Her warmth and good humor were contagious and brightened whatever activity she shared. She and Mama took particular pleasure in each others' company. Aunt Allie had made friends with a large woodchuck who lived under the main cabin. Chucky had learned to appreciate her exceptional wood stove cooking skills as much as the rest of us. He seemed to know when to show up at the kitchen door to accept from her hand samples of her culinary delicacies.

I recall spending time plunking away on a zither I found stored under the main cabin. I think Clyde or Kester had brought it from Appalachia, but I never heard either of them play it. Several times each summer we drove over to nearby Chico Hot Springs to swim and soak in the warm and hot water swimming pools. Bumpy rides by truck or car to Livingston for supplies were also a lot of fun. On one memorable visit I fell out of the back of the pickup on one of the town's main streets. I endured a ten minute wait before Mama and Aunt Allie noticed I was missing and returned to get me. Fortunately, only my pride was injured.

HELLROARING PACK TRIP

The last summer we stayed at the Snowy Range brought a special treat. My half brother Ledyard Blakeman and his bride Virginia were recent graduates from MIT in Boston. They had moved to Billings, where Ledge had accepted a position to start in the fall. They had rented a cabin for the summer on Mill Creek about five miles from the Snowy Range. Mother was delighted to have them so close. It gave me a chance to get to know Ledyard, who had not visited us in California since I was too young to remember, and Virginia, whom I had not met before. Arrangements were made for all of us to pack in from the Mill Creek area over the pass into the wilderness area just north of the Yellowstone Park boundary. Hellroaring Creek drained this large watershed.

The stories told by Mama and other Montanans often involved adventures on pack trips. I had seen pack trips departing many times from the K Bar and other ranches. Now, at last, I was going along. Pack trips such as this one, which involved transporting food and camping materials over fifty miles of tough mountain trails, were not taken lightly. A lot of planning and preparation took place. Several weeks before we were to leave, I was allowed to start using a saddle in preparation for the long ride ahead.

Aunt Allie, Kester, Mama, Ledge, Virginia, and I made the trip. Mrs. Darrow, friend of Aunt Allie and wife of the Park County sheriff, also joined us. We had four packhorses with us as we set forth on the road down to the main branch of Mill Creek. There we turned upstream on the Mill Creek road, continuing past Ledge and Virginia's cabin until we came to the trail head several miles later. The trail took us up past Passage Falls where Passage Creek and Baker Creek join to form Mill Creek. We then began our ascent along precipitous Baker Canyon toward the high pass near Mount Baker.

Within an hour we were above the timber line looking down more than 2,000 feet to Baker Creek below. I had never experienced anything like it. Our trail crossed many rock slides. In places it was hewed out of the granite sides of the canyon and was only about a foot wide. There was still snow on the peaks near us. I was amazed that the horses could keep their footing. I recalled pack trip stories that told of packhorses slipping off high trails. No one else seemed concerned, so I swallowed my fear and was careful to let my horse make his own decisions. I thought about the trail into Shangri-La that I had seen a few months before in the movie *Lost Horizons*. I pretended that the snowy, craggy peaks around us were the Himalayas and that we were braving these dangers on route to a lush hidden paradise. After what seemed to be several hours of this high altitude balancing, we finally reached the top of the pass and worked our way down to the timber line on the other side.

We followed the trail along Grizzly Creek and camped by Carpenter Lake near the intersection of Grizzly and the Northwest Fork of Hellroaring Creek. I was exhausted and saddle sore from what had been my longest horseback ride. The Hellroaring area was not at all like Shangri- La, but it did have lush meadows, sparkling lakes, and rugged peaks. And it was farther from civilization than I had ever been before. During our time at Carpenter Lake and on side trips we saw elk, moose, bears, and deer. I caught more trout there than I have at any one location

Aunt Allie and Kester Counts lead our pack train returning to the Snowy Range Ranch from the Hellroaring wilderness area in 1936.

since. It was one of the best camping experiences I can recall. There was good food, campfires, and story telling. The trip provided the chance for me to get acquainted with some wonderful people. Ledge, Virginia and I made up for having spent so little time with each other in the past. The trip back over the divide to Mill Creek seemed much shorter and less hazardous because of my increased confidence as a trail rider. What a grand way to end my last visit to the Snowy Range.

II. Youth: 1937-1943

Chapter 4 Early Teens

ENTERING JUNIOR HIGH

South Pasadena schools worked on the 6–3–3 system, which meant that after grammar school we entered the attractive and spacious junior high school for grades seven, eight, and nine. We felt we were entering big time academia. The day was divided up into periods and we had to find our way from classroom to classroom for each subject and its different teacher. At that time the school system in neighboring San Marino went through the eighth grade. Students from there joined us in ninth grade at our junior high and then went on with us to the three grades at the high school in South Pasadena.

Although there were good times and some fine instruction, my junior high days left much to be desired. I had gained a lot of weight and was sensitive about what I felt was less social acceptance than before. Although usually used in a friendly manner, nicknames like "Lard Ass," "Big Butt," and "Tubbo," intensified an image problem that was not overcome while in junior high.

Hormones were beginning to stir my adolescent thoughts about girls like Bonnie Lathrop and Sally Nason, but their friendship seemed unattainable because of my excess poundage. These feelings of inferiority were reinforced by the increased pace of social activities involving girls.

The parents of San Marino and South Pasadena sponsored many parties at private homes for the junior high age kids. I hung around the outskirts of such affairs, seldom getting the courage to dance or even talk with the rapidly maturing females. Nevertheless, I plunged into most of the new school activities with the expectation that things would get better.

Jr. High offered a variety of shop courses which I enjoyed: wood shop, sheet metal shop, and print shop. I had a head start in the last as I had been setting type in my own print shop at home for several years. My dad had built a lean-to next to our garage that had become a kind of club house for my friends and me. A friend of Papa's bought a small printing press and a cabinet of type trays from a newspaper that went out of business. He later sold this gear to my father, who installed it in our club house. So Dick Wagner, George, and I began to set type and print *The Ear. The Ear* was a hand-lettered newspaper that I had been publishing several times a year for circulation to immediate family and friends. After we got the press, I decided to increase the circulation. As it was an election year I wrote to the incumbent governor, Merriam, and told him that my paper planned to endorse his reelection. I was very proud of the prompt reply I got from the governor, thanking me for the support of my publication.

A SPECIAL FRIEND

Richard Carter was an outgoing, energetic, and thoughtful young man who had attended Las Flores grammar school. He lived in a large, beautiful home in the northwest corner of town. Like many homes on nearby Orange Grove Avenue in Pasadena, it had been designed by Greene and Greene, an architectural firm whose distinctive style helped define the Arts and Crafts era.

Rich and I shared many interests. We liked reading, sports, and photography, and spent a lot of time at each other's homes. We traveled into Los Angeles on the Red Cars to swim and work out at the Los Angeles Athletic Club. Rich was a vigorous, natural athlete whose skills at baseball and football exceeded those of most of the varsity team members. The tragedy of his life was that he was afflicted with epilepsy.

Epilepsy was then, as it had been for centuries, a dreaded and feared condition, spoken of in secret, and considered hereditary in origin. At that time it was treated with Phenobarbital derivatives, with little real success. Its major or grand mal seizures can be very frightening to those who witness or experience them. Rich's seizures were usually of the petite mal type: he would stare blankly, raise and lower his elbows in a rapid, fluttering motion, and return to normal in less than a minute. These episodes occurred several times a week. None of us who knew him well ever indicated to him that something out of the ordinary had happened.

My own inability to comfort him or acknowledge his cruel disability probably stemmed from my parents' handling of two cases of epilepsy within our family circle. I was told that Uncle Ben Beinecke, the husband of my mother's sister Agnes, suffered from the disorder. I was also cautioned not to discuss it or indicate my knowledge of his illness to anyone, particularly members of the Beinecke family. In our own home, my father's adopted sister Alice, who had lived with us during the thirties, suffered from the disorder. In both cases, my parents considered it to be inherited. On the few occasions that Alice suffered seizures in our home, I was quickly banished to my room. There I listened with trepidation to the sounds of her grand mal seizures and the first aid efforts involved. My imagination magnified such events and my level of apprehension.

One day Rich and I were exercising on the horizontal bar my father had constructed in the north east corner of our back yard. (I had outgrown the small chinning bar and swing set that I had partially painted during the Long Beach earthquake.) The bar was about eight feet off the ground and we had learned to do pull overs, in which you pull your raised legs up and over the front of the bar and end up holding yourself stiff-armed with the bar across your hips. From the resulting vantage place, the ground seemed a long way down. The dismount required tipping forward, pivot-

Richard Carter,
South Pasadena
Junior High, 1939.

ing on the bar across your middle, and flipping onto your feet as you dropped to the ground. Lacking any gymnastic training, we were pleased to have mastered this maneuver.

Rich was at the high point of this exercise when he pitched forward with a loud, terrible groan and crashed to the ground thrashing and convulsing. He was having a grand mal seizure—the first I'd ever witnessed. There was no way I could ignore or remove myself from his plight. I had learned enough first aid to know that I should try to prevent him from injuring his tongue and mouth. Overcoming my feeling of panic, I managed to get a stick between his jaws and restrain him until the seizure stopped. He appeared to be unconscious and I ran into the house to get help. Mother was there and she came out and wrapped him in a blanket and then called his mother. We phoned a doctor who arrived just before Mrs. Carter. Rich was groggy but apparently had not hurt himself in falling. Mrs. Carter took him home and within a day or two he was back in school and we resumed our good times together. From that point on we both acknowledged his illness and I was able to show my concern.

Rich will always remain a tragic, brave, even heroic figure to me. Although he suited up and often practiced with the football team, he never scrimmaged or played in a game. He could still kick and pass farther and more accurately than anyone on the team. When most of his friends went into the armed services a few years later in World War II, he was disappointed to be left out. He volunteered to be part of a group of epileptics participating in a test of a new anticonvulsant drug. He died from effects of the trial medication. Several of us were able to attend his funeral. I like to think that the thousands of epileptics, who with today's more effective medications lead normal and productive lives, owe a special debt to Rich.

THE RADIO SHOW

Dick Hucks arrived in the neighborhood about the time I entered junior high. A couple of years older than I, he was an energetic and creative addition to the street. A talented pianist and singer, he soon had us working on puppet shows and other theatrical projects. The Wagner's garage was fitted with curtains, and parents and friends sat through a variety of musical and dramatic presentations largely inspired by Dick.

Dick organized a kid's band which consisted of him at the piano, Marilyn playing the ukulele, me on the harmonica and kazoo, and two other neighborhood players as percussionist and violinist. After several spirited rehearsal sessions we were able to render recognizable versions of several classics of the period including *Three Little Fishies* and *The Music Goes Down and Around.* Our ragtag group entered an amateur hour featured on one of the less prominent Los Angeles radio stations. I recall going to the studio after alerting all possible listeners—family, friends, and casual acquaintances—as to the date and hour of our great debut.

The program's director greeted us in a friendly manner and told us to take our places with other contestants in the front rows of the studio audience. He indicated we would be called up to the stage when it was our turn to perform. After the show began, we endured a series of singers and musicians each of whom we applauded politely at the urging of the director. Finally we were called on stage to perform. Although we seemed to be doing well by our own less-than-rigorous standards, we noted that most of the audience had departed or was in process of leaving. It was not until we returned home that we learned, from those who had listened to the program, that the show had gone off the air before we performed. So much for show business.

BIRDS AND BEES

Neither of my parents made an effort to enlighten me regarding sex. My time in Montana had made me aware that animals mated in interesting and strange ways that the adults never saw fit to explain. After my grandfather died, I would sometimes go up to the office he had maintained over our garage and look at his stamps and other mementos. During one such perusal I found a medical book that described male and female human reproductive organs. There were anatomical drawings that I poured over with great interest but with little comprehension of the functions of the labeled features. I recognized the outlines of the male organs but I had never seen the pubic area of a female and had not made the connection between human behavior and the animals seen in Montana.

This ignorance was dispelled one warm summer afternoon when Dick Hucks and I went to the swimming pool at Alhambra Park a few blocks southwest of Fletcher in the neighboring town of Alhambra. I had spent a lot of time in Alhambra Park over the years with my friend George because his parents enjoyed playing tennis on the public courts there. Many of the kids on Fletcher enjoyed going to the park's plunge, the nearest public swimming pool.

The storm drain that George and I had often crossed on our backyard route to Oneonta continued south under Alhambra Road, the border between the two towns, and ran along the eastern edge of the park. As mentioned earlier, the sanky's tunnel under Alhambra Road was long and dark. On this enlightening day Dick Hucks and I decided to save a few steps en route to the pool. We climbed down into the drain to cross it at the southern terminus of its long dark tunnel. Graffiti existed even in those far off years. In the twilight zone just inside the tunnel, someone had painted in large letters several of the most common four letter expletives, all of which I had heard used, without definition, many times, mostly in Montana. We went a short way into the tunnel to look at the words on the walls and I asked Dick to explain their meaning. As he described the activity defined by the word "fuck," everything seemed to fall into place: the innuendoes and whispered jokes of Mother and other adults, the engraved illustrations in my grandfather's medical book, and the mysteries of the female anatomy. I told Dick how his information had cleared things up, and he carefully answered the many questions prompted by my new-found knowledge.

As we emerged into the summer sunlight from the tunnel, we passed a couple of young teen age girls in bathing suits, their hair wet and straggly from swimming. They were on their way into the tunnel, apparently using the storm drain as a shortcut too. We heard them shriek with amusement as they read the words on the wall. The hollow sound of their voices resonated loudly from the cement walls of the tunnel. Dick and I were dumbfounded when they began to chant, "Come on in and fuck us. Come on in and fuck us." Dick and I looked at each other and climbed quickly out of the sanky. We hurriedly made our way across the park toward the noisy crowd of youngsters in and around the swimming pool. Dick's reaction to the girl's invitation had been amusement, but mine had been fear, bordering on panic. This was not the behavior of heroines such as Bonny Lathrop or Sally Nason who I thought resided on pedestals. It was one thing to fantasize about romantic encounters, but this earthy offer to participate in the basic activity I had just learned about taxed my youthful physical and psychological capabilities.

THE BEER DRINKER

As a young teenager I tended to exaggerate when describing my Montana activities to my Southern California friends. On a couple of occasions when participating with my Montana relatives in haying or other hot summer work I had been offered and accepted a few swallows of beer. This made me feel grown up and was reported with nonchalant pride to George one afternoon at our house. "Yes, George," I said, "I drank a lot of beer last summer. In Montana they don't care how old you are. It sure tastes great when you've been working cattle or helping on the haying crew. We usually had one or two brews each day."

What I didn't realize as I made this pronouncement was that my father was within earshot in the next room. My heart sank as he entered the room saying, "Gosh, John, I didn't know you were fond of beer." I expected a severe rebuke and was surprised when he said in a serious tone, "I have some beer in the house and I would like see you drink some. I don't want to lay in a supply for you until I have a better idea of your capacity." He got out one of our folding card tables and set it up in the middle of our living room. He asked me to get a chair and sit by the card table.

Then he went to the ice box and got a quart bottle of East Side Beer, so named because its brewery was located on the east side of Los Angeles. This inexpensive beer was favored by thrifty souls like my father and grandfather. I had noticed that out-of-town guests to whom it had been served seldom commented favorably and nearly always declined a second glass. "Now's your chance to show us what a great beer drinker can do. Please stay at the table until you finish the bottle," my father instructed.

I nervously poured out a glass of the beer. It had a bitter taste that I had not remembered from Montana. With some difficulty I slowly finished the first glass. A daunting amount remain in the quart bottle. It took me about fifteen minutes to finish the second glass, and I was feeling queasy. George had left for home a few minutes before, having tired of the sorry spectacle. I got about half the next glass down before I stopped, green and on the verge of throwing up. I just sat there for what seemed like an hour, looking at the unpalatable liquid. Finally my dad returned to the room and asked, "Are you sure that you're a beer drinker?" When I replied, "I'm not," he called off the experiment. I sheepishly admitted that I had overstated my Montana consumption.

In later years, when high school, military, and college friends suggested a beer, I always declined. I still don't like the taste of the stuff.

The Telescope

Each school day, one of the periods was set aside for club or special project activities. I joined the telescope club, the chief purpose of which was for each member to build a reflecting telescope. From South Pasadena we could see the Mt. Wilson observatory, which then had the world's largest telescope. Living as we did near Caltech, where the mirror for the new and larger Palomar telescope was being ground, there was a lot of interest in telescopes and astronomy.

For an hour each school day for the next three months, I walked around a barrel shoving a four-inch-diameter disc of thick plate glass back and forth across another similar disc of glass secured to the barrel top. We bathed the interface between the discs with a solution of increasingly fine Carborundum and then rouge. Each of us in the club painstakingly ground down the concave face of the reflecting mirror we were creating. Every few days we would take the blank glass pieces off the barrel and check them with special instruments to see how well we were matching the target curve we were grinding in the glass.

I recall how upset my friend Art Krause was when he dropped his mirror blank on the concrete floor of our work area, thus wiping out several months of careful and patient work. Those of us who were more fortunate persevered to see our blanks sent to Caltech for silvering. We mounted the returned mirrors in a five foot length of the heavy cardboard tubing on which carpets were rolled in those days. It was a proud day when I took the completed telescope home, mounted on a tripod.

The telescope worked well for viewing the planets and afforded spectacular views of the moon. However, my efforts had been made with a terrestrial application in mind. I took the telescope up to the office my late grandfather had used over our garage and focused it on Marilyn Wagner's bedroom window. I discovered to my disappointment that the 4" reflector was ill-suited to the task for which it been constructed. Because of its power I was only able to see a small area of skin instead of the broader survey of femininity I had expected.

I guess this interest in the female form, which has endured to this day, resulted in part from the absence of any female siblings in my household. I had noted with interest the biological differences that shaped the clothing patterns of the opposite sex, and even before our light show, Marilyn had pointed out differences in unclad statuary to me during a visit to the Huntington Museum and Gallery in nearby San Marino during grammar school years. It was the San Francisco Fair that brought living and breathing reality to the matter.

LESSONS FROM THE FAIR

My parents had generously conceived the idea of my visiting the San Francisco World's Fair in 1939. I was given sufficient funds for a week. Arrangements had been made for me to stay with family friends, the

Markells, who lived in the Berkeley hills overlooking San Francisco Bay. I was able to ride the trolley from their house to the fair. It was held in the middle of San Francisco Bay on Treasure Island, a 400-acre landfill between the two parts of the new San Francisco-Oakland Bay Bridge.

Exotic and wondrous exhibits filled beautiful buildings. The landscaping was magnificent. Great performers like Benny Goodman gave free outdoor concerts. Many foreign countries had pavilions through which I wandered, strengthening my resolve to become a world traveler. A particular highlight for me was my first airplane ride. I used my entire budget for one day to ride in a seaplane over the fair and San Francisco. My love of flying was born that day. When I look down at the surface of our planet now, I still feel the awe that I experienced first over San Francisco.

I made a surprising discovery at the fair. I had of course been through the Gayway or entertainment area on nearly every day of my visit and was intrigued by the forbidding sign "For Adults Only" on some of the attractions. There were a number of these: *Sally Rand's Nude Ranch*, *The Folies Bergere*, and *Stella, She Moves, She Breathes*. Toward the end of my week at the fair I decided to test the adults-only restriction. A large fourteen year old, I manfully walked up to the ticket office of the Sally Rand attraction and attempted to buy a ticket. "How old are you?" I was asked. "Eighteen," I replied. "What year were you born?" My hesitancy in replying had prevented my ticket purchase, but I had learned that if I could pass myself as eighteen perhaps I could get in. Later that day I was admitted to the Folies Bergere by responding with an appropriate age and date of birth. My knowledge of anatomy took on new dimensions with that wonderful French review. I managed to get into the other two attractions before I returned home. Stella, however, turned out to be somewhat misrepresented; she was an oil painting that had been exhibited in various saloons since the turn of the century. The movement and breath trumpeted in the promotional effort consisted of a cord fastened to the back of the picture in the general area of Stella's naval. This was pulled by an unseen source to simulate a sensually heaving torso.

It was not long after I returned from the fair that I put my newfound box-office talent to use. I took the Pacific Electric streetcar in to Main Street, the skid row of Los Angeles, and gained easy admission to the Burbank Burlesque Theater. The ensuing scrutiny of the array of show girls featured there opened new vistas. Betty Rowland was the headliner, memorable as the red-haired bombshell. It should be noted that the performers were not particularly energetic at the first show which began at ten in the morning. There were some excellent comics such as Joe Yule, Mickey Rooney's dad, whose routines were classics.

I of course shared my discovery with my friends. George and I made a number of summer morning visits to the Burbank before Mrs. Wagner passed the theater on the Big Red Cars and spied us standing in line waiting for the first show. She told Ree who severely disapproved but agreed not to tell our parents if we would find other more suitable vacation activities. However, Walter Reinhold and I used some of the comic routines observed at the Burbank for the junior high assemblies. While we were still seventh graders we began to put on skits that preceded the main events of the weekly student body assemblies. I am sure the faculty members who supported our theatrical efforts would have been surprised to learn the source of our material.

THE CHRISTMAS PAGEANT

Not all of my ventures on the junior high stage were successful. The last Christmas Pageant presented shortly before our midyear class departed for high school is a case in point. Traditionally, the Christmas pageant was given twice—once in the morning at an all-school assembly and then again that evening for parents, relatives, and friends. In an era without civil rights prohibitions concerning religious presentations in schools, this particular program was an unabashedly Christian-oriented nativity show. I had been cast as one of the shepherds. Despite my tendency to sing off key when unsupported by other singers, I was to sing a duet with Jean Haverstock, who was cast as an angel.

At the morning performance all went well until our scene where the angel appeared to the group of shepherds. She materialized on schedule but as I arose from the seated group of shepherds and moved toward her, Herbie Beckman, one of my fellow shepherds, extended his shepherd crook, encircled my ankle, and caused me to fall forward in an impious heap. The audience of our peers was delighted and applauded and cheered this unforeseen event. My fragile singing confidence evaporated and the angel sang her part accompanied by hoarse squeaks and groans from me. At the conclusion of the performance a very angry principal, Verlin Spencer, gathered the cast together. He said that in the second performance the shepherd scene would be a tableau with music only—no movement or sound from the performers.

MISCELLANEOUS MISCHIEF

As an adult I have noticed that children reach a high point in outrageous behavior during the adolescent years spent in middle school or junior high. This was certainly the case among the kids I grew up with. Although drugs were not a factor then, some of the antics I observed or participated in were at the least dangerous and at the worst illegal. A few instances come to mind.

The Arroyo Seco is well known as the site of the Rose Bowl. Its dry canyon generally comprises much of the western borders of both Pasadena and South Pasadena. When I was in junior high several graceful concrete bridges spanned it to carry traffic across into the Los Angeles and Glendale areas. These bridges arched over a hundred feet above the stream bed. One afternoon I found myself with four adventurous classmates who decided to climb up the concrete arches under a bridge that carried traffic across the Arroyo Seco. We rode our bikes up to the base of the span and began the climb up the northern of the two parallel arches that supported the bridge. It was tough going at first because the lower part of the arch was almost vertical. As we clambered up with fingers and sneakers dug in, the slope decreased, and it became easier. As the climb became gentler, I realized that physical effort was not my main problem. Although I was in dead center of the six-foot-wide arch, I was becoming increasingly concerned with the distance above the stream bed.

By the time we were at the concrete crossbeam that

tied the arch to its southern counterpart, I realized that I was more frightened than I had ever been before. It appeared to be nearly a hundred feet to the ground. To my horror my companions decided to cross the crossbeam and return to the ground via the other arch. Then they proceeded to *walk* the twenty feet across the three-foot-wide crossbeam, stood on the other arch, and called to me to join them. It took what seemed like an eternity for me to inch my way across that beam on hands and knees. I grasped upper corners with white knuckled hands, as my friends laughed at my fears and urged me on. I was sure relieved when we backed down the other arch and returned to our bikes. I have never been able to completely get rid of the fear of height that I discovered that day.

At lunch time students were not allowed to leave the junior high grounds. On most days the large lawn in the inner courtyard was full of kids gathered in groups, talking, yelling and sitting around. Because of the increased interest in the opposite sex, there was a great deal of teasing and horseplay between the boys and girls. One warm spring noontime during our last year, the teasing and horseplay accelerated into a tag-like chase. An increasingly large band of the more popular and aggressive boys was running after several of the school's most mature and attractive girls. The object appeared to be to grab, hug, and kiss the girls who initially seemed to be enjoying the new game.

I hung back and watched the proceedings. At first I envied the boys who were in the chase. My feelings changed first to discomfort, then to dismay, when the spectacle turned into a mob scene. The girls had been pushed to the ground, each surrounded by a group of boys shoving forward to fondle their breasts and exposed legs. The girls were no longer laughing and appeared frightened. No one seemed to want to defend or help them. Mr. Flynn, the assistant principal, arrived on the scene and began pulling the boys away, shouting at them, "Stop! Right now!" The boys fell back and quickly dispersed. This gang grope was very upsetting to me. I had stood by and watched as several girls whom I liked were mauled. I hadn't made a move to help them. Where was my spirit of chivalry and courage? I was down in the dumps for several weeks, feeling inadequate and guilty.

A few weeks later, a less emotion-charged event occurred. The tracks of the Southern Pacific spur line that ran from Alhambra up to Pasadena ran directly behind the junior high. Since the only rail traffic was a daily freight train consisting of two or three box cars and a caboose, we paid little attention to this right of way. Each May, however, the season was marked by the passage of a circus train. We were given a brief recess to see the gaily painted cars, waving performers, and caged animals. Because there was a slight grade as the tracks climbed toward Raymond Hill, the train usually moved at a slow pace allowing us more time to enjoy this glimpse of a traveling circus.

This morning, however, the scene was different. The train moved slower and slower and finally stopped altogether. After a few minutes, it was apparent that something was amiss. We could hear the engine still puffing away a block or so north of the school. Train men and circus personnel climbed down and moved back and forth beside the train, conferring and shouting questions and orders. After a few minutes we were summoned back to class and away from the confusing show. Just before lunch hour we were told that there was to be a special circus parade up Fair Oaks Avenue which we and other townspeople who got the word could attend. Sure enough, there was a midday parade through the heart of South Pasadena, replete with marching elephants, clowns, horse-drawn cages, and carriages. What most of the spectators didn't know was that this spectacle was delivered to us by one my junior high classmates.

Harry Geyer had been planning his prank for several months. Each time he visited one of the nearby gas stations he would gather a small amount of lubricating grease or axle grease as it was known then. His horde of the slippery stuff increased until he had filled several quart paint cans that he had carefully cleaned and prepared to receive the gooey material. Verifying the Pasadena date of the circus, he rose early on the momentous day. Before breakfast and departure for school he went to the spur line and applied the grease to several hundred feet of the tracks just where they began their steepest accent. At the fiftieth reunion of our high school class Harry verified that he considered the circus train incident one of the greatest achievements of his school years.

In my early teens, I began what I recognize now as a tendency to hold back and act as an observer or judge of what is going on around me. Like others beset with negative views of themselves, my defense against possible failure or rebuff has been to disengage and criticize the people or situation at hand. In high school I was to learn that observers may see more details, but participants have more fun and lead richer lives. Now the people I admire most are those who step up, work through life's difficulties or handicaps, practice to improve, and stay involved.

Chapter 5
Growing Up Montana Style

SUMMER WITH THE LANGSTONS

Aunt Dora and her husband Jesse Langston never had much money, but they had a happy marriage. They produced five confident, active, and fun-loving kids: Little Allie (to distinguish her from Aunt Allie), Young Jesse, Phil, Cleve, and Dot. Two of their Langston cousins, Gordon and Bob, lived with them some of the time. When I was twelve I spent the summer with the Langstons at their place on Sweet Grass Creek, about two miles north of Melville. I am not sure what Mother was doing that summer but she deposited me in the middle of this easy-going brood and dropped by from time to time to see how things were going. I was pleased to be at a working ranch, out from under Mama's control.

There was much coming and going of the younger Langstons. All of them were seven or more years older than I. The white two-story ranchhouse couldn't accommodate us all. I slept in a separate platform tent house along with any of my male cousins who happened to be at home at the time.

The experience was different from my earlier ranch visits in Montana. At the other ranches, I led a relatively pampered life, protected both by Mama's zealous caution and fear for my safety and the nature of dude ranching's concern for comfort and care of visitors. At the Langstons I was fair game for any mischief my cousins could concoct.

I became aware of this the first night I retired to my cot in the platform tent. Shortly after I dozed off I was awakened by groans and moans and flashlights being shone on the sides of the tent. Suddenly two bloody hands came in under the canvas by my cot and groped toward my head. Terrified, I tumbled out of the cot and stumbled outside to find Gordon and Cleve wiping the ketchup off their hands and gleefully regarding the success of their unusual welcome.

I had to help with chores such as bringing in water, chopping wood, or feeding the hogs. There was construction going on; I assisted in ways they considered non-damaging to the project at hand. One hot sunny day I was up on the roof of the two-story ranch house while it was being painted and found that Cleve and Phil had painted all around me. I was distressed because of my fear of heights and the fact that they left after removing the ladder used to reach the high roof. If Aunt Dora had not missed me at lunch time and had them put the ladder back, I probably would have spent the day there.

One morning I told my cousins I would like to ride out toward Porcupine Butte, a couple of miles to the north. Cleve said, "John, we have just the horse for you." Peanuts was a black Shetland pony stallion. He turned out to be one of the meanest animals I ever encountered. His size was welcoming but when I got near him, I saw unbridled hatred in his dark eyes. Putting a bridle on him without losing a finger to his bared teeth was a feat requiring all the courage I could muster. There was no way I could saddle him, so it was back to the bareback regimen favored by Mama. Fortunately I approached him from the front and was quick enough to dodge the kicks he aimed at anyone who got close to him. My cousins applauded when I got aboard and survived a few desultory bucks intended to abort my trip to Porcupine Butte.

He seemed to settle down a bit as we headed across the open fields toward the ruins of Crag Eyrie, where Mother and Tom Blakeman had lived twenty years before. After about a mile, we came to a steep-sided irrigation ditch. Peanuts stopped and looked around toward me to indicate his unwillingness to continue. Taking a page out of Uncle Paul's horse training manual, I decided to show him who was master. I swung my legs out and gave him a huge kick in the ribs. Startled and angered by my surprising show of assertiveness, Peanuts bolted forward headfirst down the steep embankment into the ditch. I grabbed his mane in a futile effort to stay aboard, but slid over his head. I landed on my back in front of him in the shallow water. Most horses would have made an effort to avoid a person in their path. Peanuts deliberately walked the length of me, fortunately missed my head, and left four distinct hoof prints on my torso and legs. He then clambered out of the ditch and headed toward home at a brisk trot. When I finally trudged into the ranch-house area wet, bruised, and bedraggled, I found that my plight prompted much amusement instead of the solicitude I would have expected a few weeks earlier.

Surprisingly, I enjoyed my cousins' hazing and teasing. I liked the feeling of independence and self-reliance that the Langston clan inspired in me. Gordon especially contributed to my changed view of myself. Whenever he had a chore that I could help with he would call,"Give me a hand, partner." I was able to participate instead of acting as a guest or observer the way I had at the other ranches. As the summer progressed I was able to help more and more.

When haying began, I had a job on the hay crew. A man designated as stacker worked on top with a hay fork to arrange and compress the pile of hay that was becoming a new stack. My job was to walk beside the growing stack, hold the reins, and control the pair of horses that powered the overthrow. This device, like a big catapult, provided a means of throwing raked hay onto the stack. I felt grownup sitting down with the haying crew to the immense meals that Aunt Dora prepared for the family and outside help assembled for this seasonal activity.

Another aspect of feeling more grownup came with my attendance at the Melville monthly dances. Melville had never reached the prominence desired and promoted by my Grandmother Van Cleve. The expected railroad line connecting Big Timber and Harlowton never materialized. When sheep raising diminished, a planned woolen mill was not built. Attempts to lay out a street grid and develop and sell residential lots failed when drought, grasshoppers, and unstable livestock prices discouraged possible buyers. By the time I knew Melville the handful of buildings in the town hardly justified its continued presence on Montana maps. Bob Hart owned the dance hall. The Harts, early settlers of the area, had changed their cattle ranch into a dude ranch, the Dot S Dot, located near Melville. Diary entries left by Bob's mother, Nan, explain the Hart's ownership: "1929 — Melville dances under Driscoll too tough for guests to take." "1930 — Bob took over the Melville Dance Hall in the old warehouse."

Melville had been a rough town for most of the fifty years that preceded my arrival. Before World War I, its saloon was the scene of several shootings and murders. From what I observed from my first Melville dance, it had not completely shed its wild ways. Raised on a strict schedule of early rising and early bedtimes, I was excited to be attending this dance that got underway around ten pm and was expected to end around two or three in the morning.

There was consternation around the Langston place on the afternoon before the dance. The youngest son, Cleve, had not returned from the train trip he made to Billings. It turned out that the trains involved were freight trains. These were the depression years of the 1930s. From the highway that runs beside the Northern Pacific tracks between Billings and Livingston, it was common to see as many as fifty men riding in and on the cars of a slow-moving freight train. As drummer in the dance band, Cleve was considered an important part of the festivities. Around supper time, a message reached the Langstons that Cleve was in jail in Big Timber. He had been apprehended by the local police as he jumped off a freight. Uncle Jesse drove to Big Timber to get him out. By ten o'clock, Cleve was on hand to thump out the rhythms of *Chinatown, My Chinatown*, the current hit tune that opened the evening.

I had a great time dancing with my female relatives and observing the area's biggest summertime social event. The couples followed a counter-clockwise path with much spinning and dipping. I guess the dance pattern followed that of the horse races that were so popular at western rodeos and fairs.

The dance floor was a little above ground level and at the west end there was a kind of basement area entered from a separate entrance. A bar and eating area was set up down there. Mother was at the dance and warned me, "No children are allowed down there." From the noisy shouts and loud talk heard when the music stopped, it didn't sound too peaceful or friendly down below. During one of the later intermissions, I sneaked out and walked along the road to where I could see back into the bar area. Sure enough, amidst the drunken hubbub a fight was in progress. To my surprise, one of my cousins came hurtling out the door bloodied from his encounter. It turned out he got off lightly. Later in the evening, after I returned to the dance, another man was shot during a more violent disagreement in the bar area. This caused Mother to take me home early. Although I was disappointed, I was pleased to have stayed up past one in the morning. I had participated in what my brother Ledyard would have called "a real western event."

FAMILY DUDE

Most summers I spent some time at the Lazy K Bar, which had become one of the best-known dude ranches in the country. As I got older I began to view these visits with mixed feelings. It was wonderful being in Big Timber Canyon's scenic setting and taking part in the rides and other activities that the ranch provided for its guests. Such visitors could call themselves dudes, but I learned at an early age that family and employees were not to use the term. This label had long been applied throughout the West to belittle newcomers and those whose appearance, manner, and lack of ranch skills set them apart from the locals.

Because of Uncle Paul's generosity, Mama and I were never charged for our stays at the Lazy K. She took this as her due because she believed that her first husband's earlier investment in the ranch was substantial and never repaid. Mother spent more time there than I did. She came to be highly regarded by many of the guests who returned year after year. She relished her role as Uncle Paul's sister, a knowledgeable horsewoman, and an authentic Montana pioneer with a vast fund of local lore and ranch stories. She became a fixture at the upright piano that stood just outside the dining room in the main lodge. Most evenings a group would gather around the upright to join her in singing old time songs from her huge repertoire.

I was concerned because I felt that the Van Cleves considered me a non-paying dude rather than someone who had the ability or ranch experience to help while we were there. I would like to have wrangled or had some other job that would let me feel I was helping as a family member. One my difficulties lay in my being nearly ten years younger than the other thirteen cousins in my generation of Van Cleve relatives. It seemed to me that Uncle Paul and Aunt Helen as well as other family members considered and treated me as a somewhat effete and useless city boy. This was at odds with the view I sought to hold of myself as a courageous, vigorous, resourceful young Westerner.

My half brother Ledyard and his wife Virginia felt this same lack of respect and sense of imposing upon Uncle Paul and Aunt Helen. Some years later, after World War II, they chose to take their young children to the Hart's Dot S Dot ranch on the flats near Melville. They felt more welcome there than they had at the Lazy K Bar.

THE CATTLE DRIVE

From the time I entered my teens I increasingly spent more time each summer in Southern California and less in Montana. I did get back to the Lazy K for several memorable experiences, however. In the summer of 1940, I took part in a week long cattle drive. It involved bringing several hundred head of Herefords from some semi-arid sections about ten miles southeast of Melville back to the Crazy Mountains. There they were to graze in the summer and autumn in the National Forest land that checkerboarded the foothill and mountain area owned by Uncle Paul.

Several years earlier a guest taking part in this annual drive had dubbed the area to which we rode "No Bush." An apt title, for water holes were far apart and its brown grass landscape was treeless and flat except for rocky gullies that were not evident until you suddenly came upon them. Unlike the higher foothills and canyons of the Crazy Mountains, this barren region supported few forms of wildlife except a large population of rattlesnakes.

Uncle Paul had acquired the ten or fifteen sections in No Bush from Leo Cremer, a well-known supplier of bucking stock to the major rodeos. Cremer owned the major portion of this desolate area in Eastern Sweet

Grass County. As was true of a number of families whose lands abutted those of the Lazy K Bar, there was little love lost between the Cremers and the Van Cleves.

The cattle drive from No Bush into the Crazies was similar in most ways to much longer drives that had moved big numbers of cattle to and throughout Montana sixty or seventy years earlier. We spent several days rounding up the cattle that were spread throughout a number of sections of the desolate area. Lead cattle were designated and the more skilled punchers handled the point jobs directing the cattle toward their new pasture lands. Less experienced riders took positions along both sides of the herd and to the rear. Extra horses in the ramuda were controlled and brought along also in the rear. The noisy dirty cattle bumped, humped, and jostled each other as the riders moved the herd slowly forward. The heat, dust, and stupid behavior of the excretus-covered cattle diminished the romantic appeal expected by those on their first cattle drive.

From time to time, a steer or a cow with her calf would make a dash to get away. Then one or more riders and sometimes a dog rushed to turn the strays back into the mass of moving cattle. The sheep dogs that helped with this containment effort were impressive. They were often more effective than some of the bouncing, inept riders who fought to control their horses as they dashed over the rough terrain.

The biggest difference between this drive and those of earlier years was that trucks brought along the necessary food, cooking and sleeping gear, and supplies. Ranch hands in these vehicles preceded the riders and set up camp in the spots selected for overnight stays. When the drive reached the foothill area near Otter Creek, we encamped for a couple of days. The cattle were separated by summer pasture destination, and the calves born during the past year were branded, castrated if male, and given shots. Guests from

Lazy K Bar cattle drive. Sweet Grass County Montana, 1940.

the ranch who had not gone on the drive came down to watch and help in the branding. Punchers roped and dragged calves to the fires where branding irons were heating. The bawling calves were upended and held down while the irons sizzled the Lazy K Brand into their hides. The bull calves had their testicles cut out with a sharp knife; tar was swabbed on the wounds. Both the heifers and new steers received shots and ear cuts or tags. I had been involved in branding activities before. I was always surprised at the gusto displayed by the guests of both genders when holding down the terrified calves and the enjoyment that spectators seemed to derive from this painful show.

When the drive ended and the cattle settled in to enjoy the fine grass of their new grazing areas, we returned to the regular routine of the ranch. I think most of those who took part in the drive gained a real appreciation of the hard work and long hours of riding required to move the thousands of cattle brought into Montana during the previous century. The work continued for those early cow punchers who elected to become ranchers. They had to face the extremes of Montana weather to provide winter feed, manage calving, and move their herds to and from pasture lands. Ranchers often had to make long cattle drives to get their cattle to the nearest railroad for transport to feedlots and slaughter.

RODEO RIDER

That summer I also made my rodeo debut. At that time, an amateur rodeo was held each summer in the flats just west of Sweet Grass Creek on the outskirts of Melville. Local ranch hands and some guests from the dude ranches in the area competed in steer riding, calf roping, horse racing, and other rodeo events. On a smaller scale, it had all the trappings of the bigger shows like the Livingston Roundup. There were corrals, chutes for bucking

l load an injured calf into a truck during a cattle drive in Sweetgrass County in 1940.

stock, judges, and pickup men on horseback. A clown was in the corral near the chutes to divert angry animals from fallen participants. A public address system blared western music and amplified the corny commentary of a local announcer who knew most of the entrants. A large, boisterous crowd of spectators and the cars and trucks that brought them surrounded the fenced-in arena area.

At the urging of my cousins, I signed up for the steer riding event. It was great to amble about the hot, dusty area before my event. I wore jeans, western boots, and cowboy hat. I had a contestant's number pinned to the back of my shirt. I tried, within the limitations of my fat, knock-kneed legs, to affect the calm, swaggering look of those who had taken part in such

Virginia Blakeman took this picture of the 1936 Melville Rodeo.

shows before. I hoped I was concealing the growing apprehension that manifested itself in the pit of my stomach.

At last my event was announced. I climbed up the planks which enclosed the bucking chute and felt them shake from the thrashing of the steer who had just been prodded into this unexpected confinement. As I looked down at his broad, heaving back, he seemed huge compared to the calves that my cousins had put me on to ride in previous summers. A rope with a bell on it was pulled up under his belly and I lowered myself onto his back and fit my hand under the two ends of the cinched up rope. In my nervous state, I wasn't sure I had the strength to grip the rope. Suddenly the gate swung open, the steer humped upward, and twisted out into the arena. As he came down I continued on the original trajectory and flew in an arc, landing on my back on the hoof-torn ground about ten feet in front of the chutes. The steer never looked back as he headed for the exit gate at the far end of the arena. My rodeo career had lasted less than ten seconds. It was best described by one of my cousins who said, "John, I couldn't tell who came out of the chute first—you or the steer."

For some reason this abysmal performance didn't upset me. Although Mother was not pleased that I entered without checking with her, I think she was proud that I had given it a try. Even the kidding I received made me feel that I was now considered less of a city boy. I enjoyed the rest of the rodeo festivities and the dance that followed. When I returned to California, I mentioned casually to my friends that I had ridden a steer in a rodeo, without providing greater details of the event.

1942 VISIT

In the summer of 1942, I stopped by Montana on my way back from a national convention of the Hi–Y held at Miami College in Oxford, Ohio.

In 1942 I took this picture of four generations of Paul Van Cleves in front of the main lodge at the Lazy K Bar. From L to R: Uncle Paul, Tack, Grampy, and Spike.

Mother and I stayed at the Lazy K Bar. During the week I was there, I went on several rides, fished in Big Timber Creek, and took pictures of the ranch and family. I am particularly fond of the pictures I took of Grampy, who I was not to see again before his death in 1945. I was able to photograph all four generations of Paul L. Van Cleves together.

I also climbed Big Timber Peak for the first time. Bob, one of Aunt Helen's relatives, and I saddled a couple of horses and rode up to the high ridge south of the ranch. We followed the ridge trail up toward the peak, one of the highest in Montana. At the timberline we left our horses to continue by foot up the steep, rocky ridge that led to the peak. The route we took was relatively gentle and safe. Other mountain climbing in the Crazies was discouraged by the ranch. The predominate rock is decomposed granite that leads to dangerous footing, causes many rock slides, and makes it difficult to use regular rock climbing techniques and gear.

It is also dangerous to climb in cowboy boots whose leather soles and high heels provide little stability and purchase on the loose granite. About fifteen years before, my brother Ledyard and my cousins Harry and Spike, wearing such boots, had climbed Crazy Peak, Montana's second highest peak. Its summit pinnacles lie only a short distance from Big Timber Peak. Bob and I were climbing in sneakers, but two summers before, two guests wearing cowboy boots had attempted to climb nearby Granite peak. It is a lower peak that fills and dominates the upper end of Big Timber canyon. One of them fell and was seriously injured. He died when the car rushing him to Billings was involved in a high speed accident. My uneasiness with heights, coupled with my knowledge of the recent fall and fatality, made me proceed with great caution. With a great feeling of accomplishment, we finally stood on top and enjoyed the sweeping views in all directions. It took much less time to scramble down to where we had left our horses and return to the ranch, whose buildings had looked like dots from the peak.

Military service, college, marriage, and career intervened to prevent my return to Montana for many years. I am still discovering the myriad ways in which my childhood and youth experiences there affected my beliefs and approach to life. I know that much of my determination, ability to recognize and enjoy humor, resourcefulness, appreciation of nature, and love of animals stems from the lessons learned from Montana people and ranch life.

The main building at South Pasadena -San Marino High School, 1940. Tightened earthquake codes led to the demolition of the upper stories shortly after this photo was taken.

Chapter 6 High School

In January 1940, our class entered South Pasadena-San Marino High. The school was highly-rated academically. Most classes were well presented and interesting. There was a good balance between study and other activities. It was the other activities that made the difference for me.

SOUTH PASADENA'S MOST FAMOUS CRIME

On a warm May afternoon during my first semester, I left football practice and rode home from school on my bicycle. As I pulled into our driveway, I was hailed by Marilyn who said, "John, there's been a shooting at the high school. Mr. Spencer [Verlin Spencer, the Jr. High principal] has killed Mr. Bush and Mr. Alman. He's gone back to the junior high."

I jumped back on my bike and pedaled furiously up Fletcher Avenue and west on Oak Street, reaching the junior high in about five minutes. As I arrived on the scene I saw policemen with high-powered rifles mounted on small tripods on the raised lawns on the south side of Oak Street, facing the junior high. Without considering the hazards involved I rode my bike right through the police lines into the large quadrangle that made up the inner courtyard of the school. Small bands of students ran from building to building looking for Spencer or possible victims. I joined my friend Bill Reeder and a couple of girls. The four of us ran into the auto shop building, where I had spent those many hours grinding my telescope mirror. At the bottom of the stairs we found the body of "Chief" Vanderlip, who had been my print shop teacher. He was lying under some stored desks in a growing pool of blood. The enormity of the scene came into sharp focus for me. Feeling sick, and shocked we ran out and called to the police who quickly removed us from the premises.

It turned out that Spencer was at that time in the school cafeteria across the quadrangle. When cornered by the police, he attempted unsuccessfully to end his life with the same weapon he had used on his victims. In another room nearby, Ruth Sturgeon, an art teacher whose classes I had also attended, lay dying of her wounds. There were others dead or injured back at the high school.

The sequence of events became clear as we listened to radio news and read the banner-headlined newspapers. The board of education had been meeting in an upstairs conference room. Verlin Spencer, who had not been invited to the meeting, left his office at the junior high with a pistol he had been carrying for several weeks. He drove the three blocks to the school board building, parked in a loading zone, and climbed the stairs to the meeting room. He entered and began firing. Three were killed: George Bush, the superintendent of schools, who had held that position for many years; John Alman, the high school principal, revered by many hundreds of high school students who appreciated his kindness and high ideals; and Will Speer, the respected business manager of the South Pasadena-San Marino School District. As Spencer left the room his bullets also struck down and inflicted paralyzing injury to Dorthea Talbot, Bush's secretary, who was attempting to escape from her desk area in a room across the hall.

Spencer left the building and returned to his car. He had difficulty starting it. One of my classmates, unaware of what had transpired, helped him get the car started. He drove back to the junior high, shot the two faculty members, and seriously wounded himself.

The tragic crime profoundly affected our community. Parents and children shared a great pride in the school system. George Bush had been an outstanding superintendent of schools whose several decades of dedicated service and personal involvement in all levels and aspects of the town's educational system were deeply appreciated. The schools were closed for the remainder of the week and hundreds turned out for the memorial service honoring those who died.

The resiliency of youth asserted itself during the brief school closing. The stretch of beach at the end of Eighth Place in Long Beach had for many years been a particular gathering spot for South Pasadena-San Marino students—it was the closest beach. Even with the many stop signals on Atlantic Blvd., it could be reached in about forty minutes. I recall the sunny weekday a couple of days after the Spencer tragedy, when a Coney Island-like congestion of young sunbathers and body surfers crowded into about 100 yards of waterfront at Eighth Place. On both sides of this throng there was a mile or two of empty sand.

Spencer survived his suicide attempt and was tried and convicted of the multiple murders. The premeditated nature of his crime was clear. He had left a note for his wife Polly indicating he had planned the slayings in advance after being informed that his contract as principal was not going to be renewed. He was sentenced to multiple terms at San Quentin. There he was a model prisoner and helped plan and conduct the prison's library and educational programs. He was paroled a few years ago after serving nearly 50 years and now lives in Hawaii.

Recently a friend told me that there was an important reason Spencer did not receive the death penalty. During his trial it was disclosed that his mental state at the time might have been induced by sustained overdoses of an over-the-counter bromide medication he was taking for headaches.

EMPLOYMENT AND WHEELS

My father had encouraged me to work from the time I was about twelve when I took a paper route for the *Pasadena Independent*. It was child exploitation by the paper, which then was considered a throwaway by most of those who received it. For $5 a month I was expected to deliver it weekdays by bicycle to all the homes (approx. 200) in an area of about six blocks. Our supervisors periodically checked the accuracy of our deliveries. I remember getting critical reports specifying papers that landed in bushes, trees, on roofs, and other locations that irked homeowners. We were expected to call on each home monthly to collect a subscription fee. I guess one of the reasons I never seriously considered selling as a career was the angry response inspired by my requests for such fees.

Other jobs that I held before turning sixteen were more interesting. I worked at the South Pasadena library after school for several years. Although I mostly reshelved books, it reinforced my love of libraries, reading, and the research process. As I grew older, I spent less of the summer in Montana and was able to hold summer jobs of a month or more in Southern California. Two summers I worked in the produce department of an Alhambra branch of the Market Basket chain. (I still use the expertise I gained there when buying fruits and vegetables today.) The summer I was fifteen, I worked in the pipe yard of an oil supply company. This was the first of several day labor jobs I held before completing college. Besides developing muscles useful for football, I gained a sincere appreciation of those who support their families through such backbreaking effort.

Soon after I turned sixteen, savings from these jobs enabled me to buy, for $100, a used 1932 Ford. It was a Model B, the first Ford model to have a V–8 engine. It was a coupe with a rumble seat. Rob and Dick Wagner helped me paint the car a royal blue, complete with carefully applied cream

George Hall perches on rear bumper of my first car, the Blue Rocket,
parked in the the driveway at 2011 Fletcher Avenue, March 1941.

colored detail stripes. George and I named it the Blue Rocket. This wonderful machine opened up new horizons for us.

EASTER WEEK

In the decade before World War II, Southern California had its earlier, special version of the spring break phenomenon that later gained so much publicity in Florida resort cities such as Fort Lauderdale. Like most of the public schools in California, South Pasadena-San Marino High School closed for the week preceding Easter. All students who were able to flocked to the beaches for a week of sunbathing, socializing, and general teenage revelry. The target for our school was the shoreline in Orange County stretching from Balboa Island in Newport Beach south through Laguna Beach. Groups of girls, each generally chaperoned by a couple of mothers, rented houses by the various coves and beaches. Boys, whose housing was often less well defined or supervised, roamed the area visiting girls they knew or seeking to be acquainted with others. Hordes of nubile young women strolled the village streets, lounged in eating places, or enjoyed the warmth of the spring sun beside the chilly Pacific.

In the spring of 1941, George and I, eager to join this ritual, made special preparations for our first Easter week. We bought denim jackets and used white paint to stencil "ALCATRAZ" on the backs. We prevailed on George's aunt to help us peroxide our hair. George's came out a kind of orange color and mine a strange shade of greenish white. I am not certain what effect we expected to achieve by this outlandish alteration of clothes and appearance. Nevertheless we loaded our satchels into the Blue Rocket and set off with great anticipation for the two hour drive to the beach and its bacchanalian attractions.

Although younger and a half grade behind me in school, George was much more at ease than I around the opposite sex. His good looks and easygoing, friendly manner had favorably impressed many of the girls at high school. Several weeks before, he had told me that he was particularly attracted to Helen Bellinger, who lived down the street from us on Fletcher Ave. Helen's personality matched George's well. A tall, attractive, outgoing girl, she had told us a few days before that she would be staying with a bunch of girls at Victoria Cove, one of several small coves near Laguna Beach. George and I agreed it would be good to stop by to see Helen and her friends. We had also learned that we might be able to stay at the place that Bud Carter's parents had on the shore near Victoria Cove.

It was cool and blustery when we arrived at our lodgings. There were about ten or twelve young men who had taken advantage of the Carter's hospitality. Most of them were strangers, juniors and seniors from the classes above us. Some I recall were Bud Dickey, Bruce Hayes, Andy Armstrong, Don Royce, Evan Goltra, and Bill Herron. The last two had appropriated a nearby coastal cave for their sleeping place. Here also we met Frank Little who had moved to San Marino from the East Coast only a few months before. All were most welcoming, which buoyed my spirits by making me feel more accepted than I had ever felt during my junior high days. We stowed our gear and made for the Victoria Cove house where feminine pulchritude awaited.

I should not pass over the stowing of gear too quickly. Unbeknown to any of us, George had brought a small flask of whiskey that he decided to hide in the kitchen oven. This set the stage for a later explosion that blew the door off the oven when someone turned it on in preparation for dinner. Fortunately no one was hurt and there was no damage to the Carter's kitchen. It did make quite an impression on our new circle of older friends. I was as surprised as anyone else for, as far as I knew, George had never had an alcoholic drink.

That afternoon we found Helen, who introduced us to her friends. I recall meeting Marge Storfer, Muriel Royce, Bee Emmons, Jeanne Roberts, and several other girls. Helen seemed particularly intent on introducing us to a tall attractive girl, Mickey Magee, who she said was one of her closest friends. Mickey seemed very beautiful to me and quite beyond my expectations as a possible Easter week companion. From the glances that George and Helen exchanged, it appeared that the two of them had a much more positive belief in our compatibility. We spent most of the afternoon hanging around the house or lounging on the chilly beach. Frank Little had brought a portable record player that he set up in the living room of the girls' house. It provided a wonderful musical background to the week's activities. I tend to relate dates and circumstances to the popular music being played at the time. Our practice of singing along with the big band vocalists reinforced these memory connections. Whenever I hear *Apple Blossom Time,* my thoughts return to that beautiful cove on the southern coast of California.

Frank Little was even more polished and accomplished with the young ladies than George. His time as life guard at the country club that his parents had belonged to on Long Island had given him a tanned swimmer's physique. His sleepy-eyed, sophisticated approach seemed to bowl over the receptive young women in his new surroundings. I tended to gaze, tongue-tied, at the festivities. Both George and Frank found it easy to strike up conversations with many of the comely young women in the Easter week horde.

The most important thing that happened to me that first Easter week was meeting Mickey. We really didn't become acquainted the first afternoon. Each of us focused more on the general activities of the people with whom we were staying. I stayed close to George and Frank; Mickey spent most of her time with Helen and her other friends. A few hardy swimmers attempted to body surf in the moderately high waves, but surveillance of the opposite sex was the prevailing activity. We returned to our respective living quarters for supper, which in our case was a bang-up event.

The evening was cool with a bright moon illuminating the rough surf and creating a silvery surface to the sea when we returned to the girls' house. Frank's record player was soon playing some of the many Tommy Dorsey, Jimmy Dorsey, and Artie Shaw swing records that Frank had brought with him from the East. Boys and girls from other living groups drifted in and out of the house. Some couples that had been going together before Easter week got together, and new pairing up began. Clusters of boys bantered and joked with groups of unattached girls. George and I focused our attention on Helen and Mickey, and I found myself unusually at ease as the four of us chatted together.

Later, when some couples began dancing, George and Helen did too. I asked Mickey if she would like to dance. She declined, saying that she had a bad knee. Mustering my courage and adopting what I thought was a suave and urbane manner, I suggested that we take a walk on the beach. To my great relief and delight, Mickey said, "That would be fun."

We strolled along beside the water. I took her hand and we veered inland quickly whenever the moon-flecked breakers crashed down and moved the white edge of the water rapidly up the wet sloping sand. The feel of her hand in mine was exciting. We moved down the beach to where dark cliffs framed the southernmost part of the small cove. Big rocks offshore were sending high sprays of water as the big Pacific rollers hit land for the first time. In the moonlight it was a beautiful and memorable sight.

The sand gave way to rocks and tidal pools as we came to the southern edge of the cove. We found some large rocks and sat down to enjoy the view. The periodic rumble and roar of the surf mixed with the faint sounds of music and partying from the nearby houses. By this time, I noticed a pattern to our conversation. Mickey asked questions and I answered. She asked, "Do you know what causes the waves to break?" I replied in a serious and learned manner with a long explanation of wave theory gleaned from the physics class I was currently taking. She commented on how wonderful it was that I had such information and said, "Could you tell me how the tides work? Does it have anything to do with the moon?" My ego was soaring and I felt I had found a soul mate.

To sit shoulder to shoulder with this attractive and appealing girl stirred a strong wave of attraction. Hormones surged, giving me a shaky feeling in the pit of my stomach. I nonchalantly laid my arm across her shoulder.

My extended arm felt awkward—strangely devoid of feeling. I didn't know what to do with my floppy, unmanageable hand dangling down from her opposite shoulder. The scientific question and answer session continued as Mickey studiously ignored the inert appendage draped across her shoulders. After awhile I made a rather clumsy attempt to kiss her. She gently rebuked me, saying, "I think you're nice, but we just met today." I found this response very encouraging.

I again held her hand as we walked back to the house. It was if I had crossed over some divide between those who were "out" and those who were "in." George and Helen were not there when we arrived so we sat around talking with the others and singing with the records. Mickey apologized for her singing voice but she knew all the lyrics and sang right on key. I enjoyed singing too but with less tonal accuracy and knowledge of the lyrics. George and Helen came in a little later looking somewhat disheveled and pleased with themselves. They also indicated their pleasure at finding Mickey and me together, so obviously enjoying each other's company.

As the week progressed, Mickey and I got to know each other better and had a wonderful time visiting the nearby beaches and villages in Laguna Beach and Balboa Island. We were usually with George and Helen, who appropriated the rumble seat of the Blue Rocket for our wanderings. The evenings on the beach continued. It wasn't too long before Mickey responded to my less clumsy attempts to embrace her and willingly shared our kisses. She had wonderfully soft lips that intensified my feeling that I had found someone very special.

Mickey and Helen were juniors and George and I sophomores that Easter week. We stayed together as couples, "going steady" as it was termed, during most of the time the four of us were in high school together. Meeting, loving, and being loved by Mickey was a giant step in my gaining the positive view of myself that made high school such a golden period in my life.

FOOTBALL

Another major factor in the transformation that took place in high school was football. It had been my favorite sport from early childhood when we used to play touch football in the street at Fletcher Avenue. Papa's enthusiasm for the game intensified my interest. He had adopted the University of Southern California Trojans as his favorite team. For many of the years in the early '30s he bought season tickets in the Trojan Club section of the Coliseum, and I often attended the games with him. It was exciting sitting high up in that great stadium next to the USC rooting section surrounded by avid USC fans. I was quite young, about five or six, when I began attending. I must have found it somewhat confusing or frightening. Even as an adult I have had occasional anxiety dreams in which I find myself far up in a mythical stadium, unable to get an unobstructed view of the activity being watched by the crowd.

Papa considered Howard Jones, USC's famous coach of that era, the best coach in the country. When he listed Coach Jones' attributes it sounded like a recitation of the Boy Scout Law. On the other hand, he often characterized the opponents as "dirty players who don't believe in good sportsmanship." The polarization espoused by my father between the clean-cut, honorably coached USC players and the enemy was especially evident at the 1932 USC–Notre Dame game. The coliseum, filled to capacity for this titanic gridiron struggle, became the scene of roaring angry crowd confrontation. It was evident even to me as a child that there was more going on than rooting for a college favorite. Under Knute Rockne, who had died in a plane crash the year before, Notre Dame had become the greatest football team in the US—a symbol for Catholics across the country, demonstrating the strength and virtue of their religion. On the other hand, biased supporters like my dad were eager to see the Fighting Irish defeated just to demonstrate the superiority of their beliefs. Since he never attended church, I guess my father was rooting more as an anti-Catholic than as a Protestant. In any case, the tension and anger of the crowd at that game were more memorable than the outcome.

As I got older I became a great fan of football. I avidly followed the fortunes of the USC Trojans in the newspapers and on the radio. During my grammar school years we played touch football in a Friendly Indians football league made up of teams from each of South Pasadena's grammar schools. Our Onconta team did pretty well against all the other schools, except Lincoln Park, in the western part of our town. There we encountered Frank Stunden whose advanced age and size heavily affected the outcome. His teammate L.D. Knight demonstrated an aggressive combativeness that struck fear into our normally brave hearts. It was my first taste of team effort and I enjoyed it immensely.

The athletic program at the junior high did not include football or team competition with other schools. Those of us who liked football went to many of the high school games and looked forward to the day when we would be able to go out for football.

When we entered high school early in 1940, our midyear status meant that for the spring semester we were freshmen. In the fall our class combined with the class a half year behind us from the junior high. We became the sophomore class scheduled to graduate in June of 1943. This extra half year of high school gave us some advantages and flexibility in scheduling desired courses and, best of all, the opportunity to participate in spring football practice.

After passing the required physical exam and getting the written permission of our parents, we freshmen who wanted to play football showed up for our first spring practice. The issuing of equipment was the first big event. We had to provide our own football shoes, jock straps with protective cups, socks and T-shirts. We received heavy canvas pants with pads, shoulder pads, helmets, and practice jerseys. As I struggled into the unfamiliar gear, it seemed to me that all the upperclassmen were watching me and the other newcomers with amusement and disdain. I was, in fact, fat and not in very good condition. This was in marked contrast to the more mature, muscular, and lithe athletes all around me.

It was wonderful what dressing up in a football uniform did to my appearance and self-image. Suddenly I had broad shoulders thanks to the pads and it was not possible to distinguish between muscle and flab beneath the heavy padding of the football pants. I came to recognize in later years that I have always enjoyed wearing a common uniform with others, whether in sports, the military service, or in the buttoned-down shirts, gray flannel suits, and tan raincoat days of my business career. Even now I get a kick out of donning jeans, western shirt, cowboy hat, and boots when visiting Montana or other cattle areas of the West.

We drilled on the fundamentals of blocking and tackling. My weight, which made me too slow to play as a back, was an advantage in the line. I was out of breath much of the time and I was pushed around by much smaller players. It was apparent that at fifteen I lacked the strength, stamina, and skill of the seventeen and eighteen year olds who expected to be playing in the fall. Ineffective as I was, I still relished the idea that I was "out for football."

In late August, after a summer job spent stacking and loading petroleum drill pipe, I reported for football practice in much better shape. The team's new coach, Frank Williamson, greeted us. It became apparent that Coach Williamson, who had earned national recognition as an outstanding lineman at USC, was committed to molding us into competent players. Sam Roberts, our assistant coach, was a history teacher from Oklahoma. A former player and coach, he had also just come to South Pasadena. The two new coaches worked hard to teach us the basics of the game.

It's hot in Southern California in August and September. My chief memory of those first days of practice is of running wind sprints, constant conditioning exercises, lunging into practice dummies, pushing blocking sleds, and running more wind sprints. At the end of these grueling workouts all we wanted to do was to get out of our sweat-soaked gear and into the showers. We let the cool water run on our heads and gulped long drinks of the cascading water to restore the several pounds of fluids we lost each practice. I would bike home completely exhausted. Before long I found that I was able to run as fast most of the other linemen. Muscle began to substitute for fat. This was the beginning of a gradual weight loss that continued throughout my days in high school. I had started spring practice weighing over 210 pounds. By the end of the 1940 football season I was down to about 195. In each of the next two seasons I lost ten more pounds.

During his distinguished playing career under Howard Jones at USC, Frank Williamson had been an intelligent, aggressive lineman who learned his lessons well. A hard taskmaster and excellent teacher, Williamson spent a lot of time explaining the game and detailing his planned plays and strategy. Within a few weeks he had developed us to into a well-conditioned and well-drilled group from which he was able to field a winning team. He revitalized the football program at SPSMHS. During our three seasons, the SPSMHS Tigers used the single wing formation on offense and most of us played on both offense and defense. Like most other high school coaches, Williamson switched in later seasons to the T-formation and used separate offensive and defensive teams. He enjoyed ten years of winning seasons and developed a number of players who became outstanding college players before he left to become principal of Monrovia High School.

Although I only played once my first year I will always remember the excitement and thrill of running onto the field for the first time. It was during a night game played against Montebello at our school's big new concrete athletic grandstand, built by the WPA only the year before. The recently installed lights bathed the field in a bright golden glow. The idea that I was actually taking part in the game put me in a kind of trance. This euphoria faded only when I finally made contact with my opposing lineman.

I took great pride in being part of the varsity football squad. Few later achievements in life produced the change in self-esteem wrought by high school football. During the second season I played some time in every game. I began the third season as starting tackle beside the fearsome three R's of our line—Reeder, Reinhold, and Rose. We did well as a team and in our third year won the San Gabriel Valley League championship and went on to the California Interscholastic Federation (CIF) playoffs. There we

This practice field photo of some of our 1942 Championship team includes many friends.
L to R: Linemen: George Hall, Gene Blanche, Beni Reinhold, Steve Rose, and me.
Backfield: Bob Nuccio, Sandy McGilvray, Alan Dale, Keith Harnish, and Johnny West.

were soundly defeated by Bonita High School. Their team featured Glen Davis, who later gained fame as an All American at West Point. In the interest of complete reporting I must reluctantly add that a few months later this Bonita-South Pasadena game was featured nationally in Ripley's *Believe It Or Not*. We gained this cartoon fame because at one point Bonita scored four touchdowns in less than two minutes.

In Search of Manhood

It was in the football locker room that I became aware that I was not maturing as rapidly as most of the young men around me. During my junior high days I grew taller and as mentioned earlier became increasingly overweight. I was observant enough to note that most of my gain in height and weight was occurring below the waist. It distressed me to see that my body pattern was more similar to my mother's ample-bottomed figure than to my dad's. He had slender legs, a big chest, and broad shoulders. My sixth grade class picture shows me with legs long and big enough for someone several years older matched with a smaller upper body.

During my years in junior high I rationalized my concern with the expectation that my shape would change when I reached puberty. During the first years of high school, when I began to enjoy the increased social activities, I became worried about my immature body. I began reading about body types and had classified myself as possessing what my research indicated was a picnique or pear-shaped body. I observed in the locker room that I was not developing the larger male sex organs that seemed an important mark of maturity among my high school associates.

I determined to do something to remedy the situation. *The Los Angeles Herald-Express* that my father brought home each evening often carried, at the bottom of the last page of the sports section, some small but intriguing ads that seemed to address my problem. These tiny display ads, which the more staid *Los Angeles Times* would never have accepted, bannered HELP FOR MEN, usually with a drawing of a pretty woman. The text indicated that their establishment had medicines, devices, and various "medically approved" means of enhancing sex drive and the size of the male organ. The address was on Hill Street, a block west of Main Street. It was located in the skid row area that I had frequented before Mrs. Wagner's vigilance abruptly ended my days as a burlesque show critic.

So I boarded the Big Red Cars for another adventure in the seamier area of downtown Los Angeles. I found the address between Fifth and Sixth Streets and entered to find a dank and dark stairway, smelling of urine, leading up to the second floor. There, down a hallway lit by single light bulb dangling from a frayed cord, was a door with a frosted window marked "Men's Medical Supplies." Conquering my apprehension, I entered to find a small room with a glass counter and several display cases full of some of the most outlandish devices I had ever seen. There were also a number of books and bottles of various remedies and potions.

The proprietor was a small man who appeared to be in his fifties or sixties. He was friendly and must have dealt with other teenagers seeking the same sort of help. It was not easy to tell him why I was there, but I managed to blurt out my need. He showed me around the showroom and described the different approaches to penis enlargement in a very matter-of-fact way. Most of the devices seemed based on the premise that periodically placing the male organ in a vacuum over a period of a few months would stretch and enlarge it. I could see immediately that my solution did not lie in his collections of vacuum chambers, rubber gaskets, and vacuum pumps. I could visualize either of my parents coming into my room and seeing a large glass cylinder with a vacuum pump attached and saying, "Oh, that looks nice, John. Are you doing some sort of scientific research?

Show me how it works."

The same sort of problem existed with books. My room received periodic scrutiny from others that would make it difficult to explain the titles in his collection. We finally agreed that the answer might lie in medication. He told me that hormones affect the growth of male genitals at puberty and adolescence. He said that he could sell me some testosterone tablets that I could place under my tongue on a daily basis to accelerate the desired growth. I had run across the male hormone testosterone in my efforts to research my problem and it sounded good to me.

So I agreed and bought a small bottle containing fifty tiny tablets of what he said was testosterone. I returned home and began to take the tablets. I have subsequently discovered that this was dangerous self-therapy, but I survived the course of treatment with no appreciable effect of any kind. About a year later, I mentioned my concern to Dr. Jackson, our family doctor. After a complete physical, he declared that while small by my pornographic standards, I was within "normal" limits.

During high school and many years thereafter, feelings of this physical inadequacy, rather than any moral imperatives, ruled out the promiscuity I envied in others. In later life, however, I became more philosophical about wasting emotional energy on such matters for which solutions are not available.

WORLD WAR II COMES TO SOUTHERN CALIFORNIA

Most Americans who were old enough at the time remember where they were and what they were doing on December 7, 1941, when word came of the Japanese attack on Pearl Harbor. In the movie *Stalag 17*, the hero (played by our former Fletcher Avenue neighbor, Bill Holden) unmasked the German spy among his fellow prisoners by noting the error in time of day the Nazi infiltrator made in describing his memories of this momentous event. I am sure that not many places in the country were enjoying the bright sunny weather that we were. The sunlight highlighted the tall red poinsettias bordering our driveway where I was standing on that Sunday morning. My father was working in the garden bed between our house and the Wagners. Mr. Wagner shattered the tranquillity of the day. He came out and told us to turn on our radio because the Japanese had just bombed our fleet in Pearl Harbor.

The national excitement, shock, and anger that led to the immediate declaration of war with Japan and Germany verged on paranoia in Southern California. My father's first reaction was to remind us all that this dastardly act vindicated his often-stated suspicion and dislike of the "Japs." Many in California used this appellation to denigrate those of Japanese ancestry. Because the California Coast was closest to Hawaii, most local politicians and military officials believed that our area was in immediate danger of attack. Using the lessons learned in London, a civilian defense plan was put into effect. Within a few days we began to observe blackout rules. We put blankets over the windows of our house. Volunteer air raid wardens were appointed and trained. Illuminated signs and street lights were turned off or painted so as not to show from the air. Air raid sirens were installed and only official cars whose headlights were taped to tiny slits were allowed to drive after dark.

Walter Reinhold, Bill Reeder, Art Krause, and I, along with other high school classmates volunteered for a civilian defense rescue unit. We received a concentrated program in basic and advanced first aid as well as instruction from the fire department in techniques for extracting injured people from burning or damaged buildings.

Special passes enabled us to travel during blackouts and pass through police lines. We wore blue-gray uniforms with red cross patches. We were given helmets, arm bands emblazoned with the civilian defense emblem, and gas masks. Our unit used a station wagon converted to carry first aid equipment and serve as an ambulance. We drilled on the South Pasadena street map until we were able to locate any address in our town. As sixteen and seventeen year olds we were proud of our new found skills and contribution to the area's war effort.

The bombing or invasion that many in Southern California expected right after Pearl Harbor did not materialize. Within a month or two the area settled down and, although the blackout restrictions continued, most civilian activities returned to pre-war routines. From the news of naval activity in the Pacific, it soon seemed unlikely that the Japanese had the capability of mounting a major military effort against the West Coast.

Little changed at the high school except for one important event. By Federal edict those of Japanese ancestry had to leave their homes for internment camps and removal from California. Bill Yamanaka had been a friend and admired classmate of mine since our days at Oneonta. In the early grades at Oneonta we had known him as Masami, but he had changed his name to William to reflect his US birth and desire to be considered an American. An excellent student and athlete, his friendly manner had made him a popular student leader. Bill had been elected president of our freshman class only two years earlier.

We learned of his departure on his last day at school in January 1942. The last class I had with him was geometry, taught by Mr. Monroe, whose twin daughters Anne and Judy had also been classmates of Bill since grammar school. That winter morning, Mr. Monroe firmly established the respect and regard that many of us in that class have always had for him. He stopped our lesson to acknowledge Bill's departure. At that time Mr. Monroe was one of very few who voiced disagreement with the harsh and unfair decision to uproot and imprison these Japanese-Americans. He was near tears as he told Bill and the class that it was a tragic day when frightened government officials could do this to our community of Nisei friends. He said Bill was one of the finest young men he had ever taught and expressed his profound sorrow and concern over his enforced departure.

Ben Reinhold and Art Krause saw Bill once shortly after the war, when I was not in Southern California. But it was to be fifty years before I was to see Bill again. He did not attend any of the high school reunions and none of us knew his whereabouts or what he had been doing. Beni Reinhold finally made contact with him from leads provided by some of our other Nisei classmates. In the fall of 1994, Ralph Wood, Beni Reinhold, Art Krause, and I made a special visit to Tucson for an emotional reunion with Bill. I finally had the opportunity to see him and convey how much I admired him. I hope I adequately expressed the regret I have felt for not expressing my friendship and bidding him a proper farewell on that sad day fifty years ago.

In the early morning hours of Wednesday, February 25, 1942, a few weeks after Bill's departure, Mother woke me from a sound sleep saying, "John, wake up. The war has come—you have to get to the rescue unit." My room at that time was a kind of sun porch, upstairs on the southwestern corner of our house. Through the many windows, looking toward the center of Los Angeles, I could see a panorama that indeed looked like an air raid. Searchlights were probing the skies and antiaircraft batteries were firing from many locations. The recently installed air raid sirens were sounding and the bright flashes and rumble of the exploding shells added to my certainty that a major air attack was underway.

Donning my rescue unit uniform and grabbing my gas mask and helmet, I said a brave good-bye to Mother and rushed downstairs and out of the house. Jumping on my bike, I pedaled up Fletcher Avenue and headed west on Oak Street to Fair Oaks and on up into the center of South Pasadena to our Rescue Unit headquarters. It was a memorable ride through the blacked-out streets with the sight and sound of anti-aircraft activity continuing. Several police cars and new Civilian Defense wardens challenged me en route. I found most of my friends in the unit when I arrived and we spent the next few early morning hours awaiting rescue dispatches that never occurred. The air raid sirens finally signaled "All Clear" and we returned sleepily to our homes just before breakfast time.

I expected the raid to be featured and explained in the press, but nothing appeared until Wednesday evening. Then the evening papers reported that Secretary of the Navy Knox had held a press conference in Washington, saying that the whole thing had been a false alarm. Further confusion resulted when the Friday morning editions of the *Los Angeles Times* carried a front page story about an Army report that Secretary of War Stimson had just made public. The report stated that as many as fifteen planes operated by enemy agents may have flown over our area during the episode. It said further that the unidentified craft may have been commercial aircraft flown over to spread alarm, disclose anti-aircraft gun positions, and test the effectiveness of blackouts. No bombs were dropped, there were no casualties, no planes were shot down, and no army or navy planes were in action. Stimson indicated that the report had come from General George C. Marshall, Army Chief of Staff. There were other articles in the same editions reporting politicians' outrage at Knox's "false alarm" comments. There were pleas for a unified defense command, and demands to locate the bases in northern Mexico from which the planes were assumed to have flown. After a day or two there were no further press stories to provide more facts or verify the true nature of the dramatic event.

In the half century that has elapsed my curiosity has not abated.

During an East Coast visit in 1991, I talked with a former neighbor in Stamford, Connecticut, Ed Miller. He had recently completed and published a book on US diplomatic and military strategy leading up to the early months of World War II. I asked him about the Southern California "air raid." He said his research had indicated that it was not an enemy action. I told him I had read newspaper accounts of the period, quoting Secretary Stimson as presenting a contrary view. Ed suggested I check with the Military Records Section of the National Archives in Washington, D C. I contacted Ed Reese there by phone. He listened to my questions and called me back a few days later. Reese cited references indicating that Chief of Staff, George Marshall, had briefed FDR on the matter on February 27. The transcript of the briefing showed that Marshall's investigation led to the conclusions released to the press by Secretary Stimson later that day. Except for a hilarious movie *1942*, issued many decades later, which lampooned the events of the early morning pyrotechnics, I have never seen reference to the event or an explanation of what actually occurred.

A few weeks later a Japanese submarine surfaced offshore north of Santa Barbara and shelled some oil tanks and pumping equipment. This act received far more attention in the national press. Except for some balloon-carried incendiary devices released at sea later in the war in an effort to destroy timber in the Northwest, no further enemy attacks occurred on the Pacific Coast.

My Parents' Divorce

During those early months of the war another important event occurred. Shortly after the holidays my dad went away on what I assumed was a business trip. Mother asked me to come upstairs where we sat in my parents' bedroom and talked. She had been crying, her voice was wavering, but she came right to the point. "John I'm sorry to tell you that your father and I are separating. For the next few weeks I will stay here in the Fletcher house with you. Then I'll be going to Reno to spend the required time for a Nevada divorce. We have agreed that you will continue to live with your father until you finish school." It was difficult for me to respond. I finally blurted, "Why?" She said my father had asked Aunt Allie to get her to agree to the divorce because he was very unhappy in the marriage. She said, "I'm sorry to break up the marriage, but I don't want to stay together if he feels that way."

My first reaction was anger at both of them. After a short while, I realized that it didn't make much of a difference to me. I settled down but continued to feel some mild regret and what I guess was embarrassment because of what I perceived to be the stigma attached to divorce. I had observed for a number of years that my parents didn't seem to take much pleasure in each other's company. I had enjoyed being with them individually and I knew how much each of them cared for me, so the break was not difficult for me to take. When Mother returned from Nevada she rented a small bungalow on Fremont Avenue, near the high school. I dropped by to see her frequently as did George and a number of my other friends. When school was out, she moved to Bozeman to live with Aunt Allie.

In August my father married Marion Buckley Ingersoll, the widow of Don Ingersoll, who had been at the Union Oil Company before his death a few years before. Marion was a bright, attractive, gray-haired woman with two high school age children. Ward, my new stepbrother was about my age and his sister Janet was about two years younger. They were three nice people and, although we all felt a little uncomfortable in our new relationship, we got along well together. Dad and Marion found a two-story stucco house for rent on Milan Avenue, only two blocks away. So in the fall we moved from the house on Fletcher where I had lived for nearly fourteen years. Ward stayed with friends in Whittier to finish his senior year in high school and Janet transferred to SPSMHS.

SPRING OF 1942

As the days got warmer and longer, the high school again returned to much of its pre-war spring pattern. Friday noon dances were held in the patio behind the school auditorium. The fancy of many of us turned as seasonally expected to the opposite sex. For Easter week, Mickey and Helen stayed with a group of girls on Balboa Island. George and I talked my father into allowing us to use the Brown house on the tip of the Newport-Balboa peninsula. This spacious two-story home had a commanding view of the channel into Newport Harbor. It was built in the middle twenties for Chester Brown, a senior executive at the Union Oil Company. Mr. Brown had been my father's mentor and friend for many years before his death in the late thirties. I recall many visits to the Brown house as a small child. The wonderful views and opulent life style of its occupants impressed me. I remember in particular the Chinese cook, who fussed over me and was always able to produce some unusually tasty oriental snack or delicacy. My father had agreed to be executor for Mr. Brown's estate. He was in frequent contact with the surviving family members, all of whom had taken up other residences after his death. They agreed that George and I could stay in the furnished and maintained house for Easter week, with the understanding that we would not entertain there or bring in others.

Though it was not as memorable as the watershed Easter week of the year before, we had a great time. There was much less driving around and more time lounging around the beaches on Balboa Island and the ocean front on the mainland. George and Helen were as much fun as ever and Mickey and I had become closer and more relaxed with each other. I don't recall whether we told the girls of the injunction against visitors. However, when they asked to see the sumptuous quarters we had been describing, we readily agreed to show them "the fine view of the harbor entrance." Fortunately the happy afternoons and evenings the four of us spent in the place did no damage to the house nor to our relationships with the girls.

Mickey's warmth and beauty had captivated me from the start. Her quick and retentive mind became apparent as I got to know her better. She was willing to apply a great deal of energy to whatever task she undertook. She sought to disguise her intelligence by asking others for their ideas, rather than stating opinions of her own. She seemed to want to avoid social situations and didn't appear to want to meet or deal with new or aggressive people. Sometimes we would drive up to a party or other get-together and she would not want to leave the car to join the gathering. This shy side of her nature was hard to understand for she had so many appealing facets to her.

Her tremendous willpower and ability was evident during the annual Copa de Oro assembly. The Copa de Oro was the high school yearbook. Mickey had served on its staff during her sophomore and junior years and been elected its Editor for 1942. She did an excellent job of managing the design, layout, and execution of the book. She and her staff combined text with hundreds of photos of people and activities to create an exceptional record of the 1941–42 school year. Each year the editor acted as MC for a spring assembly that featured awards and commentary on the past year. Mickey expressed great concern as to whether she could handle such a public presentation. She then proceeded with great charm and aplomb to conduct an outstanding assembly with no script or notes whatsoever.

I became interested in drama activities about this time and joined the Peter Pan Players, who put on several productions each year. In my first role I played the hero in a one-act melodrama, *Blackout*, set in wartime England. This timely potboiler had to do with unmasking a Nazi spy. The student audience liked it. Connie DeRidder, a beautiful and popular member of our class, played the female lead. I had often admired Connie from afar. A measure of my rapidly growing confidence was my ability to execute with assurance and pleasure the on-stage embraces and kisses with this attractive young woman.

An even bigger production was *Black Flamingo*, a costume piece dealing with intrigues in a pre-revolutionary French royal court. Many of my friends played more important roles. I played Popo, a prissy court fop who pranced about chasing a plump chambermaid, delivering my lines in a falsetto voice. Popo's clownish behavior contrasted with the more serious parts played by the hero, heroine, villain, and other court characters. It was clear that the audience didn't recognize me at first in the long curly wig and fancy costume. Not all those attending were favorably impressed. At spring football practice, the afternoon after our evening presentation, Coach Williamson looked at me with some distaste and said to the assembled players, "Well, here's Popo."

Each spring semester the school held spirited elections to choose from the junior class the school officers for the following fall. Rather than having student body president, vice president, treasurer, etc., six commissioners constituted the elected student body officers. My friend Walter (now called Beni) Reinhold, president of our junior class, could have been elected to any of the commissioner's spots but his grades had dropped below the required level for candidates. He offered to act as campaign manager for my effort to become commissioner of interior. I was surprised at the level of support he was able to create. Bud Carter, who had developed great lettering skill by working in his father's sign painting business, agreed to help. He created the large posters that were an important element in SPSMHS

High School Students Choose Seven Commissioners

Newly elected commissioners for South Pasadena-San Marino Senior High School for 1942-43 are pictured above as follows: (Left to right) Dick Vanderhoof, commissioner of finance; Barbara June Kellow, commissioner of publicity; John Church, commissioner of interior; Martha Peterson, commissioner of correspondence; Sandy McGilvary, commissioner-general; June Rogers, commissioner of sales promotion, and Frank Frericks, commissioner of athletics.

political campaigns. The most effective sign we developed was patterned after the inscription over the entrance to the Earl Carroll night club in Hollywood. Over the door to the girls' gym that opened onto the courtyard where the students gathered at noon we placed a sign that read:

> **THROUGH THESE PORTALS PASS**
> **THE MOST BEAUTIFUL GIRLS IN THE WORLD**
> **Courtesy of John Church**

My opponent in the election was Dick Jones, a good looking, popular student, fellow football player, and friend who had been vice president of our class for both the sophomore and junior years. I thought he would win. On the day before election Beni and many of my close friends contacted all their friends. They suggested that those who supported me wear white shirts and neckties to school on election day. The result amazed me. A large proportion of both the girls and boys in the departing senior class and in our junior class arrived wearing this special attire. It seemed to do the trick and for the first time in my school years I was elected to a school-wide office. I don't recall any subsequent event that boosted my view of myself as much as seeing all those kids wearing white shirts.

SUMMER OF 1942

In June, shortly after school let out, Ralph Wood and I represented our local chapter at the national convention the Hi-Y held at Miami College in Oxford, Ohio. Ralph was another close friend who had been a classmate since kindergarten. For both of us, this was our first trip east of the Mississippi. The train ride gave us a chance to become acquainted with other California delegates. The convention held on the beautiful campus was lots of fun. Our California delegation nominated me as a candidate for national president of the Hi-Y, but this political bid was less successful than my high school campaign a few weeks before. Ralph and I stopped over in Chicago on the return trip and visited the Loop and business district of what was the largest city we had ever seen. We parted company there. Ralph returned to Southern California; I took the Northern Pacific to Montana for a brief visit.

When I returned home I went to work again in the produce department of the Market Basket store in Alhambra. I spent most of my spare time with Mickey who was preparing to depart for Stanford in September. By this time I had become close to her family. Her father and mother were fine people who had come to California from Missouri in the early 1920s. When I showed up at their home on Lorain Road in San Marino, they were always friendly and welcoming. I had also come to have great regard for her sister and brother. Barbara was a couple of grades behind us in high school and Dick was in junior high at the time. Mickey and I spent many romantic evenings in the Magee's living room. The rest of the family discretely provided for our privacy by occupying other parts of the house.

As we had during the previous summer, we often went on double dates with Helen and George. The University of Wisconsin had accepted Helen and she would also be departing in the fall. We enjoyed occasional excursions to the beach and nearby mountains and saw many movies together. We went on several occasions to the Palladium in Hollywood. There, along with multitudes of kids in our generation, we reveled in the music of the great bands of the swing era such as Tommy Dorsey and Glen Miller. This year, because of gasoline rationing, most of our dates took place close to home.

In the last weeks of the summer Mickey and I began to discuss how our impending separation would affect us. We decided that each of us would enjoy the coming year more if we were free to date others. I was somewhat apprehensive about the effect on Mickey of what I assumed was the superior charm and romantic appeal of the college men at Stanford. At the same time I harbored fantasies of applying my new-found confidence around young women during the coming senior year at SPSMHS

FALL SEMESTER

After Mickey had departed for Stanford, I threw myself into the many activities that began with the start of the school year. Sandy McGilvray, the newly elected commissioner general, held a get together of the new commissioners at his home in San Marino. I knew some of the others quite well. June Rogers had lived close to me on Fletcher Avenue. Martha Peterson and I had been in many classes together in junior high and high school. Dick Vanderhoof was a friend from junior high days. Sandy, Lewie Simpson, and I had played football together. Among those I knew less well was Barbara June Kellow, whom I had admired for some time. BJ, as she was called, was a friendly, pretty girl with beautiful and expressive brown eyes. During Sandy's party and later meetings of the commissioners at school, I found myself strongly attracted to BJ. I asked her to dance at the Friday noon dances and she seemed delighted to accept. She was a real pleasure to be with. As the fall semester progressed, I found myself seeking her out and we had some wonderful talks. Since most of our class assumed that Mickey and I were a couple, BJ always asked about her and how things were going at Stanford. During these chats I learned more about BJ's family. They lived in a large home on St. Albans Road in San Marino. Her mother had taken over the family printing business and was reportedly doing an excellent job. The large residence, the fine clothes BJ wore, and the late model convertible she drove to school were indications that her family was well off. BJ also had a serious suitor, Clark Cornell, who had just completed his flight training in the Air Corps.

In retrospect I recognize that one of Barbara June's most compelling attributes was her unfailing empathy and warmth toward others. At the time however, my ego assumed that her wonderful receptivity to me indicated she was equally attracted to me. We attended a couple of school functions together and had a lot of fun. However, when I dropped over to visit her at home for the first time, I sensed that there were major obstacles to what I had assumed was a ripening relationship. Chief among these was her mother. Mrs. Kellow answered the door to find this grinning newcomer who asked to see her daughter. It was immediately evident that Barbara June had not inherited her empathy and receptivity from her mother. After a cool survey of my appearance and the 1932 Ford at the curb, she asked me to identify myself. After what seemed a long decision-making period, she asked me to enter. When BJ appeared the three of us went into the spacious living room. A stilted conversation of about fifteen minutes followed. BJ was her usual friendly self, but Mrs. Kellow assumed the role of interrogator.

Her questions reflected little interest in me and seemed aimed at bringing Clark Cornell into the following exchange: "Have you met Clark?" —"No." "Has BJ told you that they expect to be engaged soon?" —"Not exactly." "Did you know he has just received his pilot's wings in the Air Corps?" — "Yes, BJ told me." "Don't you think the country is lucky to have young men of his caliber in the service?" —"Oh, yes." It seemed clear to me as I drove away from the brief call that Mrs. Kellow had her mind set on Cornell as a son-in-law. One of BJ's close friends told me soon after that Cornell had worked summers at the Kellow's company. She said Mrs. Kellow was grooming him to take over the family business after the war.

My attraction to BJ was causing some confusion as to my feelings toward Mickey. The letters Mickey and I exchanged reflected no diminishing of affection by either of us. It did occur to me, however, that if separation could lead to the fickle emotions that stirred me, perhaps Mickey might be experiencing similar feelings and ideas up at Stanford.

During this period another significant event took place—Marilyn got married. About a year and a half before, the Wagners had moved from Fletcher Avenue into a new house in San Marino, not far from the Huntington Library. Marilyn and her brothers had been away at school or work. Except for a brief stint that George and I put in pulling weeds out of the Wagner's new lawn, I hadn't seen much of the family since their move. I was surprised and honored when Marilyn called to ask me to serve as an usher at her wedding. She was marrying Fred Raymond, a young Naval Officer stationed in the area. I had met him earlier at the Wagners. I was impressed by his warm personality, quick intellect, and the interest he showed in me and my activities. At the wedding at the Wee Kirk O' the Heather Chapel I felt adult in my tuxedo showing family and friends to their seats and standing up front as part of the ceremony. Although I thoroughly approved of her choice, I did feel a few memory-induced pangs of jealousy. This nice guy was marrying the girl that for many of my early years I had assumed I would wed.

The fall days seemed to race by with most of my attention (and much of the student body's) focused on our successful football team. We always wore our letterman sweaters to school on Friday, the big day of the week. Excitement began to build at the eleven o'clock assembly. Each week's program concluded with a rousing game rally. The band played. Cheerleaders led the audience in school songs and loud cheers that reverberated throughout the big auditorium. The day's game was also the main topic of conversation at the noon dance held in the patio behind the auditorium. We played home games in the afternoon or evening, with large crowds in attendance. After the evening games, most of the team, either with dates or in bunches of young men, would pile into cars to make the rounds of any parties that might be in progress. We often headed for LaBrie's or other drive-ins where post-game celebrations of other high schools were also underway. There was a belligerent exhilaration, rowdiness, and cama-raderie to these Friday nights that was seldom equaled in later years.

The most extreme example of post-game enthusiasm occurred after the Covina game. The previous year South Pasadena and Covina had both come to the final game of the season undefeated and Covina had won a hard fought game 14-13 to become league champs. This time we Tigers of South Pasadena took major revenge for that loss with a 46-0 massacre. After the game Beni Reinhold, Sandy McGilvray, and I decided that we should share this wonderful result with our friends (football players and girls) from the previous class who were at Stanford. Sandy's current girl-friend Ginny Soper and his brother Don were both at Stanford, which gave him added incentive to make the ten hour drive. After telling our parents that we going to Stanford for the weekend, we took off. Around four in the morning, we pulled up in front of Roble Hall, the freshman women's dor-mitory at Stanford.

We were happily unaware of Roble's strict curfew designed to encour-age night study and reasonable bedtimes and to protect girls no longer under parental control from the perils of extended or late night dates. To announce our arrival and alert our hometown friends, we stood below the front windows and bellowed a loud chorus of a unique SPSMHS fight song. Its melody and spell lyrics came from *Constantinople*, a moderately popular song of the 1920s. By the time our high decibel efforts had ren-dered "South Pasadena, S-O-U-T-H P-A-S-A-D-E-N-A," lights began going on all across the front of the two-story building. During the next few minutes of yelled conversation with girls at the open windows two things became apparent. First, it doesn't thrill first year college women to see high school boys whose appearance clashes with their effort to present a mature image to their new classmates. This is particularly true when the loudly delivered message of such visitors has to do with a high school football victory. Second, the campus police consider early morning serenades inappropriate and disruptive behavior. As these policemen shooed us away, we managed to arrange to get together with Mickey and Ginny for breakfast later in the morning.

When we met at the student union, the girls' friendly welcome indicated that they had forgiven our embarrassing arrival. Mickey and Ginny recruited Sylvia Snow, one the freshmen girls at Roble, as a companion for Beni. The six of us enjoyed a great weekend. We attended a football game and then went into San Francisco for a seafood dinner at Fisherman's Wharf. Ben's performance at the dinner table was memorable. With a gusto like Henry the Eighth as portrayed in Hollywood banquet scenes, Ben tore into the pile of cracked crab placed before him. Using both hands, greasy with the butter into which he had dipped the crab, he stuffed the delicacy into his mouth with noisy grunts and exclamations of pleasure. The tablecloth and floor around him were soon littered. The rest of us watched this spectacular display of gluttony in speechless wonder. After dinner we wandered around the city for a couple of hours before driving the girls back to make the Roble curfew.

In the time Mickey and I spent alone together we talked about what we had each been doing. It was obvious that she was having a wonderful time. She enjoyed her classes and had made many new friends. She casually mentioned that she'd had a couple of dates with a Gordon Farrar from Alhambra. I told her that I was enjoying the fall semester at high school and had gotten to know BJ better. She knew BJ from their time together on the high school annual and agreed she was a wonderful girl. I think both of us were withholding the true dimensions of our attraction to our new friends, but our feelings toward each other seemed as strong as ever. Before Sandy, Ben, and I departed the next morning for the long drive south, Mickey and I had warmly indicated our continued love. We both looked forward to being together again when she returned home for the Christmas holidays.

The chief difference between the fall semester and those which preceded it was the war. A massive US military and industrial mobilization was underway and this war effort began to influence all our lives. Uniforms were everywhere and many of our friends and family were in the service. Porter Bruck, a classmate and student officer, had died a few months before in the Marines' invasion of Guadalcanal. Most of the news in the papers and on the radio reflected increased US involvement in the world-wide conflict. The chief topic of conversation among those of us in the senior class was when and what branch of the service we would enter. I took a competitive exam given in Los Angles for appointment to West Point. About three hundred high school seniors took the test; I was not one of the two selected.

An Army Air Corps announcement on the bulletin board outside the principal's office outlined a program being put in place at a dozen colleges and universities across the country. Applicants with college degrees in science or math were eligible to apply for admission to six-month-cadet training programs leading to commissions as weather officers. College students without science or math degrees and high school graduates were eligible to apply for an intensive one-year college pre-meteorology program focused on math and physics, completion of which would lead to entry into the weather cadet program. West Coast schools for the pre-meteorology program were Pomona College in nearby Claremont, Reed College in Oregon, and the University of California in Berkeley. Ben and I applied.

In early December the Air Corps accepted us subject to a physical exam and our completion of high school prior to the February 1 starting date. The high school agreed that our mid-year status gave us sufficient credits for graduation. Our class would not officially graduate until June. I still enjoy telling people I was a high school drop out.

On December 30,1943, my birthday and the day after Ben's, we went to the selective service office at Fair Oaks and Mission and shortened our expected senior year by signing up for induction.

III. Military & College: 1943-1947

Chapter 7 Local Soldier

INDUCTION—FORT MACARTHUR

January 7, 1943, a few days after our eighteenth birthdays, Beni Reinhold and I climbed aboard a Big Red Car bound for the army induction center in the Pacific Electric central station on Main Street in Los Angeles. There we joined about one hundred draftees from various parts of Southern California. The group contained men of various shapes, sizes, and ages. Although many were teenagers like Beni and me, some were in their mid-thirties. We lined up to take the physical exam that preceded the swearing-in ceremony. Those who failed this rather thorough physical were given a 4F rating and dismissed. The rest of us were herded into a big, dingy room overlooking the rail yards. The winter sun, shining through windows yellowed by age and grime, cast a golden glow on the rough lines of men. We attempted to follow the instructions of a sergeant who finally shaped us into an appropriate formation. An officer appeared. He had us raise our hands and repeat after him the oath by which we became privates in the US Army.

Those who have served as enlisted personnel in the armed services will not be surprised to hear that the manner in which we were treated underwent a significant change at that point. The sergeant, who until that time had guided us in a friendly and courteous manner, switched to his command mode. He called us to attention and said that meant to stop talking, stand erect with our feet together, arms at our sides, and face straight ahead. He told us to leave single file, pick up our travel kits, and assemble by the Big Red Cars that were to take us to Fort Mac Arthur in San Pedro.

As the electric street cars sped south toward the Los Angeles harbor, I remembered the many times I had ridden this route as a youngster. For four summers beginning when I was nine, I had spent a week at the YMCA camp at White's Landing on Catalina Island. These Red Cars had transported the young campers to the terminal in Wilmington where we boarded the large white steamship that made the trip to Avalon. This time the train branched off at Dominguez Junction and continued on the spur line through San Pedro to the MacArthur reception center. The fort dated back to the days when the Spanish had maintained a presidio there. Its name honored General Arthur MacArthur, father of the more recently famous Douglas MacArthur. Among his many achievements, the elder MacArthur had commanded the army forces in California earlier in the century.

We were not thinking about such history as the unfamiliar atmosphere of our first military base engulfed us. We were first sent to a warehouse for uniforms. The volume of clothing we received surprised me. It took a big barracks (duffel) bag to carry it all. We received a heavy overcoat, a dress blouse, pants, and shirts, all olive drab and made of wool. This basic color was repeated in a formal billed hat, overseas cap, wind breaker, underwear and socks. We also received cotton khaki shirts and pants and caps for summer wear, raincoats, and green fatigue work uniforms. We were issued two kinds of shoes, mess kits, a gas mask, miscellaneous belts, buckles, and insignia. Bored noncoms threw these items across a counter to us after quickly guessing our sizes.

Staggering along under the burden of the heavy duffels, we marched to our barracks. Soldiers along the way heckled us and called out insults related to our physical appearance and obvious lack of military training. At the barracks we were turned over to a sergeant who said we were the saddest looking group he had ever seen. He assured us in a loud voice that he would change that. He took us into the barracks and told us to select bunks. Army blankets, sheets, and pillow cases were issued and we received a lesson in making beds. He told us to put on our fatigues and fall out in front of the barracks. There he explained the routine of the base and the bugle calls that would shape our schedule. We then spent about an hour of drill, learning basic commands, before we marched to the mess hall for lunch.

We spent the next couple of days drilling, taking batteries of tests, getting our immunization shots, and attending classes on military protocol and courtesy. We had gas mask drills, calisthenics, and work details such as "policing the area" (picking up cigarette butts and other bits of litter) and repainting the white rocks that delineated paths and roads. Beni and I learned another important military lesson at the evening formation on our second day. The sergeant asked if there were any men present who knew all the words to the Star Spangled Banner. Ben and I and about ten others raised our hands. He then asked those with hands raised to fall out of the formation. We were turned over to a corporal who marched us to the mess hall for KP (kitchen police) duty. For the next few hours we labored in the steamy kitchen washing dishes and pots and pans. We had discovered a basic GI maxim—never volunteer for anything.

When the weekend arrived, we unexpectedly received passes extending from Saturday noon until Sunday evening at six. We surprised our friends and families who had not expected us back in their midst so soon after our departure. My dad was particularly proud and pleased to see me in uniform and insisted on taking several photos of my still-civilian-friend George and me. We visited a lot of people who seemed very interested in Beni's and my stories about our first days in the service. I unabashedly basked in the new attention that reflected a general wartime appreciation of the military. When we returned to our barracks Sunday evening we learned that we were to be transferred the next day to the Army Air Corps Basic Training Center at Fresno.

BASIC TRAINING AT THE FAIRGROUNDS

After about a six hour bus ride we arrived in Fresno, in the great San Joaquin Valley in the middle of California. I had visited this large agriculture center a number of times with my father, but had never been to the county fairgrounds in the southern part of the city. As the bus drove through a gate in a ten-foot fence topped with barbed wire into the race track area we saw the converted stables that were to be our barracks. This was not a typical army base. We had moved into what had been a few months before an internment center for the Japanese-Americans removed from their West Coast homes early in the previous year. The dirt floors of the barracks and primitive sanitation facilities vividly indicated the concentration camp nature of our Nisei friends' confinement. What a shock it must have been for fastidious families like the Yamanakas and Konabashis to have been forced from their well-kept homes into conditions like these.

Our initial reception was similar to that we had experienced at Fort MacArthur. A tough-talking sergeant met us and told us that he was responsible for changing us from civilians into soldiers. Bunks were assigned in the barracks and we again received bed making and cleanup instructions. At the morning assembly, our sergeant read us the base rules and schedule and told us to read the uniform requirements, training schedules, and duty rosters posted each day. He told us that the barracks would be inspected frequently. To receive passes and avoid extra KP or guard duty each of us would have to keep his sleeping area in perfect order. He expected the bed made tight enough to enable the inspecting officer to bounce a coin off the blanket. It was tough to see how we could keep the dirt-floored barracks area neat and clean.

After morning mess, we were issued Springfield rifles. We began to learn the manual of arms using these venerable weapons. The base parade and drill ground was the large fairground parking lot. We spent several hours a day marching or jogging around the big asphalt area. We learned to strip down, clean, assemble, and fire the Springfields. I was disappointed to discover that I had not inherited my mother's sharpshooting skills. I did however qualify with the weapon, one of the requirements for completing basic training. There were calisthenics and long marches around the Fresno area. I was glad we were there in January rather than in summer when temperatures in the Central Valley are often over 100 degrees Fahrenheit. The winter rains, however, turned the stable area into a sea of mud, making it difficult to keep our sleeping quarters, uniforms, and equipment clean. To make matters worse, epidemics of meningitis and influenza hit the base and filled the base hospital with sick soldiers.

The harsh military discipline provoked a wide range of reactions. Most of us griped and grumbled but went along with the program. However, there were several men in our barracks who became upset by the rough manner in which the noncoms applied military orders and constraints. They wasted an inordinate amount of mental energy fighting the system. These unhappy draftees seemed to draw more guard duty and KP time than the rest of us for minor infractions. The often-repeated army adage, "When being screwed is inevitable, relax and enjoy it," seemed to bring them little comfort. For the most part, I thoroughly enjoyed the idea of being in the service. It felt good to be wearing a uniform, receiving food and housing, and letting others run my life for a while.

The meteorology program for which we had signed up was to start about February 1. When that date rolled around we were still going through basic infantry type training: drilling, taking weapons training, doing guard duty, and slogging around with rifles on bivouacs and patrol exercises. We checked at Company Headquarters and they said their records showed nothing regarding an air corps meteorology assignment for us. With visions of military careers in the ground forces looming, we conveyed this distressing news to our families during our next phone calls home. Two days later Mr. Reinhold and my dad arrived at the base. With confidence stemming from their maturity and my father's army experience, they visited the base commander to determine why the army was not honoring the agreement under which we had volunteered. Our base CO put them in touch with the Air Corps Western Training Command Headquarters which informed them and us a few days later that they would keep their commitment.

About this time, the commanding officer of our company learned of Reinhold's training as a boxer. Beginning at age fourteen, Ben had spent many hours training with Bob McAllister, the boxing coach at the Los Angeles Athletic Club. On the occasions when Rich Carter and I went to the club to work out, we had often watched Ben's sparring sessions. We saw him develop into a skilled amateur who had sparred with a number of professional fighters. At the time we were at Fresno, it was an army tradition for each company to select several boxers to represent it in contests with other companies. A heavyweight match was arranged with another company, with Reinhold as our representative.

A large crowd attended the fight. A ring was set up in the parade ground area. I was dismayed when Beni's opponent climbed into the ring. Private Jones was a large, muscular man. He moved well and towered over my friend. He looked capable of inflicting permanent injury. When the fight began he lunged toward Beni and began throwing punches. My friend kept his guard up and danced back, circling this ominous adversary. The crowd was noisy, urging the fighters to mix it up. They became impatient when Reinhold continued to back pedal and watch his opponent over the top of his gloves that he held protectively in front of his face. The yells and jeers stopped suddenly when Ben jabbed with his left and caught the other man on the side of his head. Jones looked at Reinhold with surprise. The first round ended soon after, with no further blows landed by either fighter.

At the beginning of the second round the action increased. When his opponent came toward him swinging looping punches, Beni danced to the right, stepped in close, rotated forward on his left foot, and put his weight behind a left jab that rocked Jones's head back. He followed with another rotation that delivered a powerful right punch to the midsection. Jones doubled over. It was clear then that Reinhold had more training and experience. Jones continued to throw punches but he had obviously slowed down and was hurt. Beni moved in again with a combination that began with a right to the body followed by a left hook to the head that caused the large man's knees to buckle. Jones stood in the center of the ring looking hurt and bewildered. I think Reinhold expected the referee would stop the fight. When the referee and the crowd urged them to keep fighting, Beni danced up beside the man and drove a hard right to his body that caused him to crumple to the canvas. The referee counted Jones out to end the fight. I was greatly relieved by the outcome and very proud of my friend's courage and skill.

His exhibition was even more remarkable when later that evening Ben came down with what appeared to be flu or meningitis. He was sent to the hospital. Unfortunately, he was still there a few days later when we finally received word of our transfer to Pomona College to begin the pre-meteorology program. The army doctors at Fresno decided that Reinhold was too sick to make the trip and had his transfer canceled. The bus taking those of us who were going to Pomona loaded right in front of the base hospital. I remember how forlorn Beni looked as he walked with me to the hospital entrance and stood there in his blue hospital robe and waved as the bus left without him.

PRE-METEOROLOGY PROGRAM

It rained during most of our bus trip south. The rain stopped as we were approaching the college that lies at the base of the San Gabriel mountains in Claremont, California, about fifty miles east of Los Angeles. The wet, fruit-laden orange groves around the campus sparkled in the sun. The cleansed air sharpened the spectacular view of the close-by mountains and snow-covered Mount Baldy. The contrast between this scene and the dismal conditions we had left was the first indication of how fortunate we were to be assigned to this location.

A small liberal arts college, Pomona was one of twelve US colleges and universities whose academic standards led to their selection to participate in the Air Corps' meteorology training program. Pomona's president, Dr. E. Wilson Lyon, had selected Dr. Roland Tileson, former professor of physics, as academic head of the program. Working under curriculum guidelines developed by the University of Chicago, Lyon and Tileson had recruited or assigned the required teachers and staff. In just a few months they prepared the college to receive us. The basic idea of the pre-meteorology program was to provide in a year's time the equivalent of three years of college courses to prepare us for the advanced meteorology program. Upon successful completion of the Pomona program we were to go on to the advanced cadet program, given at Caltech. When we finished there we would receive commissions as weather officers in the Air Corps.

When we unloaded our gear from the bus and found our assigned rooms in Clark Hall I realized that our accommodations were first class even by non-military standards. Clark Hall was a Spanish-style complex of one- and two-story buildings. Attractive plantings complemented its patios, arcades, stucco walls, and red tile roofs. Each living unit consisted of two nicely furnished rooms with a connecting bathroom. I joined the three privates who were to be my suite mates for the next year and we agreed we had dropped into the lap of luxury.

Al Chlavin, my roommate, was from Los Angles and, like me, had come into the program directly out of high school. George Kelsey and John Pruett shared the room on the other side of the bath. George had been a student at Pasadena Jr. College, and John, the oldest and by far wisest of the four of us, had majored in history at Louisiana State Normal College. I soon discovered that they and the other 250 young men who arrived during February made up a remarkable group, ranging from university graduates to high school seniors. Most of the arrivals had at least a year or two of college work. Military preparation also varied. Many of us had just completed five weeks of basic training or had transferred from other western military bases. A sizable proportion, however, had come to Claremont directly from induction centers such as Fort MacArthur. They had only a few days of exposure to the army approach to things.

At our first formation on the evening of our arrival, our commanding officer, Lieutenant Claiborne, greeted us. As we were to learn, he was a stern but fair military professional. He turned us over to Staff Sergeant Potter. It was a surprise to encounter in this serene campus setting the same loud, in-your-face drill sergeant approach we thought we had left behind us in basic training. Those of us who had endured this time-honored military harassment before felt superior to our comrades straight from civilian life. They listened in awe to his harangue on becoming soldiers, not "college boys."

Sergeant Potter then dismissed us to go to dinner in nearby Frary Hall,

Air Force meteorology detatchment roommates at Pomona College, 1943.
L to R: Privates Al Chlavin, John Church, John Pruett, and George Kelsey.

where we were to take our meals. There we received further evidence of how fortunate we were to be at Pomona. Most of the dormitories at the college used the large oak-paneled hall as their dining center. Our detachment filled about a quarter of the long oak tables in the spacious dining area. An impressive mural by Diego Rivera covered one wall.

Many of the diners in the hall were attractive coeds. From their friendly interest in the uniformed newcomers, it appeared that feminine companionship might not be too difficult to obtain. A long cafeteria serving area along one side of the room displayed what proved to be excellent food. As we went through the line I saw to my surprise that Sally Nason, one of my most admired friends from South Pasadena, was among those serving the food. It seemed to impress my new military classmates that I knew this beautiful woman and that she greeted me so warmly. During the meal several other girls I had known in high school came over to say hello as my new roommates and others showed puzzled interest in the female attention I was getting. That first evening I established a reputation in the detachment as a ladies' man. I saw no reason to correct this false impression in the months that followed.

My strongest overall memory of the time at Pomona is of the strenuous study required. Before the official program began on February 22, each new arrival was assigned to a study section for a review of math through algebra, trigonometry, and geometry. After the program began we experienced twelve months of intense academic pressure. First a week of high school algebra, then a week of college algebra, then the equivalent of a semester of college trigonometry, presented in three weeks. When five weeks of the course elapsed we took the first government screening exam covering only elementary college algebra and trigonometry. Quizzes along the way had enabled the Pomona faculty to transfer what they deemed the bottom thirty–five students to the pre-meteorology course at the University of California that was just starting. My friend Beni Reinhold joined the beginning class there when he returned from a sick leave granted by the Fresno Basic Training Center. Our detachment was now at its target level of 220. Most of us approached the exam with trepidation. It was a great relief when only two men failed the test and were shipped out to other air force assignments.

After the concentrated five week math review, our curriculum broadened to include analytical geometry, physics, physical geography (my favorite course), American history, composition, and speech. We undertook a new branch of mathematics every few months. Unfamiliar information, particularly in the so-called core courses of math, physics, and analytical geometry was being thrown at us fast. I felt I would never be able to pass the quarterly GI exams. These fearsome ordeals focused on these "big three" subjects. This concern about my difficulty in grasping the material intensified each time one of the screening exams approached. I was fortunate to have John Pruett in our living unit. His quick mind and patient willingness to tutor his suite mates enabled me to squeak by the math tests. During the year quite a few members of our detachment were not so fortunate. The difficult exams eliminated them from the program. Each quarter's exam results showed Pomona at or near the top in each subject tested at the twelve participating colleges and universities. It became apparent that we had both an outstanding faculty and an exceptional group of students.

Apart from the fifty hours of scheduled class and study time each week, Pomona presented great opportunities for fun and recreation. We received invitations to attend and participate in many of the college activities. For the first few months we were the only military unit on the campus. With an increasing number of male students away in the military or other war efforts, the coeds who remained made us feel especially welcome. Movies and other campus activities gave us a chance to relax from our rigorous academic, physical, and military program.

After being confined to the campus for our first six weeks, we began to receive weekend passes. This was particularly good news for the 70 percent of us who lived within 50 miles of Claremont. Most Saturdays we got out in the early afternoon and didn't have to be back until 7p.m. Sunday. During my stay at Pomona I often returned to my hometown. I participated in farewell parties for many of my high school friends like George Hall, Art Krause, and Sandy McGilvray as they enlisted and left for the service. As the months passed I noted increasing puzzlement tinged with some resentment, on the part of some parents and others who observed my continued presence in the area.

One person who made my time at Pomona especially enjoyable was Marjorie DeVeau. Her sister Dianne had been in my class in high school but I had not known Marge, who had graduated the previous June. She introduced herself to me one evening at Frary Hall. The angora sweater and dark plaid skirt she wore complemented her light brown hair and attractive figure. As we talked it became apparent that this smiling, friendly girl knew many of the principal players in my life. She and Dianne were close friends of BJ Kellow. Marge also knew Mickey and many of my other San Marino friends. I asked her to go to a campus dance with me. We had a great time together and soon became regular companions at movies, concerts, and other campus events.

It was an unusual friendship. We were attracted to each other but constrained by her unique knowledge of my close relationship with Mickey and my strong interest in BJ. I came to have great regard for Marge's wise and optimistic view of life. Her compassion and supportive attitude encouraged me when I was concerned about my academic survival. We

*Our Meteorology Detachment is shown practicing a mass
calisthentics program later presented in the Los Angeles Coliseum, 1943.*

enjoyed long talks in which she told me of her family's ranch near Escondido and of her great love of horses and outdoor activities. She was an up-to-date source of information on BJ's activities and impending marriage. During the second half of the year, when her sister Dianne went up to Stanford, Marge became another channel of news about Mickey's campus activities. When we were hugging and kissing ("necking," in the parlance of the forties), I was sure sorry this warm and shapely friend's information bank and sense of appropriate behavior stopped us short of greater expressions of passion.

Physical conditioning was important in the Pomona program. We spent two hours, six days, a week in a structured athletic program that included a half hour of calisthenics followed by military track, gymnastics, volley ball, boxing, or wrestling. Military drill continued. During the August week between the second and third quarters we spent three days at Santa Anita at the firing ranges qualifying with various weapons, manning targets, and marching around the nearby foothills. The detachment then made a grueling sixteen-mile uphill march from Claremont to Snowcrest near the 10,000 ft. summit of Mount Baldy for an overnight bivouac. Next morning our CO told us that three day passes would be issued upon our return to our Pomona quarters. We were dismissed and told to return by foot at our own pace. Most of us jogged down the miles of steep road. I made it back by noon to begin a happy but footsore few days with Mickey, who was home from Stanford for the summer vacation.

John F. Curry, commanding general of the AAF Western Training Command, inspected our detachment. He gave us high ratings for the appearance of our quarters, military drill, and in particular for the precision of our calisthenics. On Labor Day, we served as General Curry's honor guard at the Los Angeles Coliseum. It was the graduation ceremony for cadets from the advanced meteorology programs at UCLA and Caltech. As a prelude to the ceremony for the new weather officers we put on an exhibition of marching, singing, and calisthenics. Our efforts were enthusiastically received by the audience, which included my father and my new stepmother, Marion. We repeated this Coliseum performance at the opening football game of the season between UCLA and USC. For this effort the detachment received passes to the rest of the season's football games held in the Coliseum.

After the departure of about ten percent of the detachment who failed the second quarter GI exams, we settled into the fall routine. Our new CO, Lieutenant DuBois, relaxed our schedule to allow one night a week off to enable us to enjoy the increasing number of campus events and local movies. By this time I had become more relaxed about my chances of survival and was better able to handle the school work. I was able to spend more time enjoying weekends at home and campus dates with Marjorie. The only cloud on the horizon was the persistent rumor that the advanced program for which we were preparing was going to be discontinued.

This scuttlebutt proved to be true. A reclassification board from the AAF Training Command headquarters arrived on campus in October to bring the bad news. Because of an unforeseen surplus of weather officers, the advanced program was being closed. All pre-meteorology students would be reclassified into other programs after graduation in February. We were asked to indicate our first three choices from a list of alternatives. This list included cadet programs such as flight crew or electronics, college programs in engineering, and various enlisted specialties such as aircraft mechanic or weather observer. Like most of my classmates I opted for the cadet programs that could lead to an early commission: my first choice was communications; second, air crew. My third choice was engineering.

In November, I survived the third quarter government tests. In spite of the uncertainty about our next duty, the spirit of the detachment remained high. We continued to study hard in our final quarter to make sure we completed the program successfully. During the holiday season I caroused with friends home from college or on military leaves. I spent Christmas with Mickey and her family. On the following weekend I was able to attend the Rose Bowl, which wartime had changed to a contest between USC and the University of Washington. I then returned to Pomona for an intensive three week review for the final tests.

In early February the test results were posted. I found that I was eligible to graduate from the program. Mickey came down from Stanford to attend the graduation ceremony held on February 12. At that time we also learned of our reclassification assignments. My orders included a ten-day leave, after which I was to report to Santa Ana Army Air Base for air crew screening and classification. I found that 95 of my classmates had received similar orders. It developed that anyone who made air crew one of their three choices had received the same classification. Several of the other men in the detachment had orders sending them into communications training. Most of the rest went to weather observer school.

I was sorry that none of my roommates had made choices that led to their being assigned to Santa Ana. I had come to admire all three of them. We had many good times together. I had spent a remarkable year with stimulating people in an exceptional college setting. It would be several years before I fully appreciated the academic benefits that the Pomona faculty had bestowed upon us. I did realize that my coming military assignment would be a lot different from the sheltered life we had led on the Claremont campus.

As Mickey and I spent a couple of days visiting our families and friends in South Pasadena and San Marino, we celebrated my good fortune in receiving another assignment close to home. Mickey had to get back to her classes at Stanford so we took the train together to Palo Alto. I went from there to Berkeley to visit Beni who was completing the pre-meteorology program at Cal. He was able to spend only a short time with me because he was under the same academic pressure that I had experienced at Pomona. When I saw the big buildings and urban setting, I was thankful that I had gone to the smaller and quieter campus. I went on up to Sacramento to visit Ree who was working at McClellan Field as an aircraft mechanic. The next day it took me about ten hours to hitchhike back to South Pasadena via US 99.

I spent the balance of my leave (an inappropriate term in my case) with my family and whatever friends were still around. George and most of my high school classmates were in the service or away at school. The most significant thing that occurred was the sale of my car, the Blue Rocket. It was taking up space in my dad's driveway and it was unlikely that I would need it for the next several years. I found a buyer through an ad in the *Pasadena Independent.* I received $250 for the old Model B that I had bought three years earlier for $100.

SANTA ANA ARMY AIR BASE

Nowhere was the massive buildup of US air power in World War II better demonstrated than at Santa Ana Army Air Base. Only two years earlier its site was covered with bean fields through which I had traveled many times to Newport-Balboa and other south coast beaches. Our group from Pomona joined thousands of young men in the process of being screened, classified as pilots, navigators, or bombardiers, and receiving preflight training at this sprawling air base without an airfield.

We were assigned to Squadron 6, made up of those who were to go through the screening and classification process. We were housed in a traditional two-story army barracks, one of the hundreds on the base. We stowed our gear in footlockers at the ends of the bunk beds that filled the main sleeping areas. It was clear that this was a no-frills, highly disciplined, military situation. A noncom informed us as to what flight we would be in and selected some temporary noncoms to assist him in shaping us into formation for drill and movement around the base. We marched off to a classroom auditorium where Lieutenant John Weaver, our squadron CO, welcomed us. In his indoctrination lecture the message was that we were an important element in building the strongest air force in the world and the days ahead would be demanding and tough. He conveyed a sense of urgency and pride about the Army Air Force and the mission of SAAAB that convinced me that air crew training was the right choice for me.

We received a booklet, *Prelude to Victory,* that amplified Weaver's message. It described the classification, preflight, and flight training programs that lay ahead. A few paragraphs from this booklet will reflect its wartime message, quite different from our weather training and our prior concepts of wild blue yonder training:

> The illusion that our near-sighted enemies of Nippon couldn't hit a billboard with a shotgun, and that our Nazi foes were a bunch of mechanical robots who couldn't think for themselves, has been pretty well dispelled by the realities of modern warfare. Our enemies are killers and your object is to get them before they get you. In this kind of warfare, Mister, there is only one paramount law: KILL OR BE KILLED!
>
> You must work hard and you must work fast. You have been selected and you will be classified and trained, to become an important national asset. You must be fit to fight. You must fight to survive. You must get to your objective and YOU MUST GET BACK.

Discipline builds strong and hard fighters. The going is tough. You are starting on a rigorous physical training program. . . . But it's a hundred to one that you'll come out of it fit as a bull terrier and ready to lick twice your weight in Japs. . . able to bounce off a fast-moving truck, turn a somersault, and land on your feet. . . Taught to shoot—and shoot straight—with rifle, pistol and Tommy gun.

The pamphlet went on to describe the two-week-long period of classification during which we would be subjected to batteries of written tests, interviews, physical exams, and tests with mechanical gadgets and equipment designed to measure dexterity and coordination. According to the brochure, these tests and machines enabled the Air Corps to determine which air crew job each of us was best suited to fill. My scores and profile were interpreted to classify me as a navigator.

In my case this was probably the proper assignment because I had some difficulty with the mechanical dexterity measuring devices. In a high school shop course I had learned to operate a metal lathe. I got rather confused when the testing device at Santa Ana had one of the positioning cranks work in the opposite direction from that on machine shop equipment. It did seem strange however that ninety of us from Pomona were classified as navigators and only two as pilots and one as bombardier.

Several weeks elapsed after our classification and before we were transferred into the preflight program for navigators and assigned to a navigation squadron. We spent this time in drill, weapons qualification, water survival training, physical conditioning, and participating in mess management, the Air Corps' euphemism for KP. Mess hall duty by any other name is just as sweaty.

Finally we began preflight school. We were promoted to the rank of aviation cadet and assigned to Navigator Squadron 94, commanded by Lt. P. H. Kiel. The Air Corps dramatized our increase in stature by raising our pay from $21 to $75 per month. We received new uniforms and insignia and slept in better barracks. We began using the cadet mess halls where the food and service were far better than we had received as enlisted men. In a time of stringent rationing, we found ourselves enjoying steaks and other menu items that were wartime rarities.

Discipline became even more rigid. At Santa Ana it was enforced by issuing demerits for barracks or drill formation infractions. Those receiving demerits were assigned disagreeable jobs such as guard duty or latrine detail, or were required to spend hours walking tours. Such tours required marching silently back and forth between two points during weekend or other non-duty hours in full dress, with a rifle on the shoulder. Cadet officers did much of the inspection and awarding of demerits.

Preflight training proved less difficult than the Pomona pre-meteorology programs from an academic, military, and physical standpoint. My increased confidence must have been apparent: I was appointed as one of the squadron cadet officers, something that had not occurred at Pomona. I jeopardized this status on several occasions when I failed to wear my dog tags, had a dirty belt buckle, and left some articles on my bed during inspections.

I was scheduled to walk tours one weekend for the demerits involved when a message came from base headquarters. Major Dwight Minton, the prereflight school CO had asked several of us cadets to be overnight guests at his home at Balboa Beach that weekend. Our commanding officer, Lt. Kiel, was as puzzled as I at my inclusion and arranged for me to defer the tours until the next week.

Thus John Meredith and Audly Clark, the two highest ranking cadet officers of our squadron, and I found ourselves Saturday in the midst of the Minton family in their large home overlooking Newport Harbor. I think Major Minton had singled out our squadron because of its parade ground precision. (A few weeks later we earned the Base E Flag, awarded to the best marching unit at Santa Ana.) I think the major invited me because of my name. Major Minton had inspected our squadron a week earlier. It had been my responsibility to call our flight to attention and announce "Flight A ready for inspection, Sir. Cadet John Church reporting." It developed that Church was the maiden name of Major Minton's wife. The major's first name reflected his mother's maiden name, Dwight. The family business, Church & Dwight, founded by their ancestors in 1846, made Arm & Hammer Baking Soda, the nation's best known brand of sodium bicarbonate. Major Minton had been an executive in the company before entering the Air Corps.

The Mintons were cordial hosts. Mrs. Minton, and her daughters referred to me as Cousin John. We spent a relaxed afternoon on the beach and strolled along the boardwalk on the shore of the bay. I knew the area well because I had spent a lot of time in Balboa as a youngster. After an excellent and convivial meal, we went with the Minton girls and a friend they had invited for the occasion to enjoy the dancing at the nearby Balboa Rendezvous. The dance pavilion, which overlooked the ocean beach, featured a well-known swing band of that era. We returned to the base Sunday morning considering ourselves fortunate to have experienced the thoughtful hospitality of the Mintons.

Life as an aviation cadet in wartime Southern California was surely enjoyable. Most weekends we had "open post," meaning we received passes running from Saturday morning until Sunday noon. Although my continued presence in my hometown was embarrassing, particularly

*Our squadron at Santa Ana Army Air Base, 1944. Shown here with
the base E Flag awarded after each Sunday's base review to the
squadron judged to be the best marching unit.*

around people whose relatives were off fighting the war, I enjoyed the good will generated by my air corps uniform. Besides the many cadet friends from Pomona, a lot of South Pasadena friends in the service were around. Lewie Simpson was in the Navy program at UCLA. George Hall, Art Krause, and Sandy McGilvray had arrived at SAAAB a few months after I did. Usually in groups of two or three we took full advantage of the many canteens and service centers in the area. I recall visiting the Hollywood Canteen. Several of us were called up on the stage to join the film celebrities who performed for the noisy and enthusiastic crowd of service men and women. One weekend some of us served as extras in some scenes at the Santa Ana airport for the film *Winged Victory.* Although none of us had been around an airplane yet, we were issued flight gear and parachutes. We played the part of flying cadets waiting anxiously by an air corps runway at night for a classmate overdue from a training flight.

The emphasis at Santa Ana was on developing us into mature and tough flight crew members. I felt I was making progress in that direction. However, an incident occurred that served to remind me that I was still in my teens and had not entirely forsaken childish ways. One open post week-end Ree came down from Sacramento and was staying with Mrs. Ranke, who lived across the street from our former home on Fletcher Avenue. On Saturday afternoon Ree and I drove to nearby Arcadia to see Aunt Dora, who was living with her son Cleve Langston and his family. Like Ree, Aunt Do was employed in a defense industry job. I found the tales they swapped about their war work interesting and impressive. These women were successfully handling skilled mechanical jobs considered the exclusive province of men only a few years earlier.

As we drove back to South Pasadena I asked Ree if she would bake one of her fabulous butterscotch pies. On Sunday morning I went over to see her at Mrs. Ranke's and she presented me with the pie. Many years earlier my cousin Harry Dugro had outwitted my half-brother, Ledyard by taking such a pie into his room, locking the door, and devouring it all. Recalling this incident, I overestimated my digestive ability. Except for two small slivers delicately eaten by Ree and Mrs. Ranke, I consumed the entire pie.

Shortly thereafter, three of my former Pomona classmates, Skee Salisbury, Randy Randolph, and Ray Schirm, who were also cadets at SAAAB, arrived as planned to provide a ride back to the base. My stomach felt a little uneasy on the drive but I made the squadron formation preceding the Sunday review. This was always an impressive weekly event, where scores of squadrons passed in precise formation before the base commanding officer and several thousand spectators.

Our squadron had marched only a block or two toward the parade ground when severe stomach cramps doubled me over and forced me to drop out of the moving formation. The squadron moved on and an ambulance arrived to take me to the base hospital. The diagnosis was appendicitis and they began to prepare me for emergency surgery. When I finally told them of my overeating, the medical staff was not amused. Fortunately they stopped their plans for surgery and sent me back to my barracks. One doctor had voiced his opinion that they should go ahead and operate to teach me a lesson. Thankfully I did not wash out of the aviation cadet program for what would have been a unique reason—gluttony.

As graduation from preflight training approached, Mickey and I realized that after a year and a half of military service within Southern California I would soon be departing for more distant and perhaps more hazardous duty. We had maintained an increasingly more affectionate correspondence and visited each other as our schedules permitted. When she came home from Stanford in June, I proposed to her and she accepted. We both liked the idea of being engaged and proudly showed our friends and families the modest ring I had given her.

I wish I could remember more clearly what our feelings were at the time. Both of us believed that courtship, engagement, marriage, and children were part of a normal and expected progression. This included education and career for the man and education, short term jobs, and homemaking for the woman. I believe the idea of such a script or plan was more ingrained in Mickey than in me. I certainly anticipated and perhaps fantasized the sensual aspects of marriage. For many couples the war affected the timing and sequence of such events. My current view of that far-off time is that neither of us understood the commitment involved or the importance of truly loving ourselves and our mate, not just loving the idea of marriage.

On June 26, we graduated from preflight school. The featured speaker was Colonel Robertson, the base CO whose main theme seemed to be "I love boys." His message did not relate to the tough "kill or be killed" emphasis promoted in our class sessions. His benevolent headmaster approach had us looking at each other wondering if our CO had dropped in from another world.

Our status didn't change after this graduation. We spent the next three weeks drilling and won another E Flag. We bivouacked in the hills behind Newport Beach, practiced Morse Code, and fired carbines, submachine guns, and 45 caliber pistols at the oceanside firing ranges. I visited with George, Art Krause, and Sandy McGilvray, who were in bombardier preflight on the base. Extra passes enabled me to spend more time with Mickey. Finally in the middle of July we received word that we would take our advanced navigation training at Hondo, Texas. On July 22 we left on a Southern Pacific troop train, bound at last for the wild blue yonder.

Chapter 8—In Western Skies

NAVIGATION TRAINING

Two days later, on July 24, we found at ourselves at Hondo Air Base, about 45 miles west of San Antonio. The heat and humidity captured our attention first. The effort required to gather our gear and get it into our living quarters left us bathed in sweat. Relatively flat, scrubby landscape surrounded the base that lay in the northern part of a large cattle-raising area wrested from Mexico during the Texas war for independence. Many of the West's major cattle drives in the last century involved cattle raised in this part of Texas.

Visually our new base was not impressive. Only the air strip control tower, a large water tank, and some silo-like structures were taller than one story. The design motif of the other buildings seemed to be south Texas tar paper. It was a relief to find floors in the long, low buildings that served as our barracks. The latrines and showers were in separate buildings, perhaps in deference to local rural custom. Air conditioning was not in widespread use at that time; it took us several days to become used to working and sleeping in the unaccustomed heat.

Fortunately the prospect of flying and learning to navigate overcame any physical discomfort or concern about my surroundings. We were assigned to a squadron and flight. Our flight CO was Lt. Williams and our instructor, Lt. Pribyl. Like most of our instructors at Hondo, Pribyl had flown a combat tour of bombing missions in Europe. Friendly and articulate, he received our close attention and respect. Our navigation equipment was issued the day after our arrival and we began classes in preparation for what was to be a series of ground and flight missions. The equipment included a chronometer, an accurate flight wrist watch, an E6B circular slide rule and vectoring device, and a bubble octant for celestial observations. We staggered back to our barracks carrying a weighty assortment of volumes including navigation tables, Air Almanac, and USAAF Navigation training manual. We also received the measuring and marking tools used by navigators everywhere: pencils; dividers; and a plastic tool to measure units of distance and angles, and draw parallel lines.

The classes, instructors, and training missions at Hondo introduced me to navigation, which has remained an abiding interest. There is something fundamentally satisfying about being able to determine where you are and where you are going. I believe this need for knowledge of one's location and direction is basic to many of life's situations. The methods and knowledge presented at Hondo derived from centuries of practice of this ancient science. Aerial navigation must be done more rapidly than ocean navigation since the speed of the aircraft and high altitude winds can affect location much faster aloft than on the earth's surface. Many years later I enjoyed applying what I learned during those months in Texas to ocean sailing. Today satellites have made it possible to determine, almost instantly, within a few feet, one's location anywhere on the globe.

At the time of World War II, however, bomber navigation required close attention and painstaking effort. Before each mission, course directions and distances had to be marked on aerial charts. We learned the three principal methods used by navigators to determine and record the plane's current position. First and most basic was pilotage, looking at the ground below and recording the time we passed over landmarks we recognized on charts (maps). Secondly we used dead reckoning in which we calculated and plotted the distance traveled by multiplying time by speed and factored in the effect of the wind's speed and direction. Thirdly we learned to calculate a "fix" showing our location. This was done by calculating and plotting the intersection of lines of position obtained from terrestrial or radio bearings, or from celestial observations using the octant. Effective navigators usually applied a combination of all these methods.

Our training centered around preparing for and flying a series of both day and night missions out of Hondo. We got to know the landscape of Texas quite well. Unlike preflight, the pressure to avoid washing out (failing) was intense. About twenty training flight missions had to be successfully completed before the silver navigator wings were awarded. Cadets were eliminated from the program if they received two unsatisfactory flying mission ratings. Ground missions were also "flown" in navitrainers, housed in the large silo structures we had noted on our arrival. These multi-storied units were for that time truly remarkable. Planetarium-like domes simulated sky conditions above for celestial navigation. Moving pictures of the surface below simulated moving terrain, altitude, turning points, and targets. These enabled the student navigators to calculate aircraft speed, wind drift, and ETAs (estimated time of arrival).

The first big hazard to my success was air sickness. I had occasionally been carsick as a child when riding over winding mountain roads. Many people experience motion sickness when reading, writing, or trying to do close calculations in a moving vehicle that is swinging through changes in direction. We flew our training flights in two-engine AT 7's whose cabin area contained four navigator stations. Each station had all the instruments needed to determine direction, altitude, and air speed as well as a drift meter to view the ground below to gauge wind effect. The bowl-shaped covers of our compasses served an additional purpose, that of the airsickness bags provided on commercial air flights. The interior of the AT 7's

This remarkable photograph shows Hondo navigation cadets on a night training mission in an AT-7 over Texas in 1944.

always carried the odor of vomit from the many cadets who got sick. Over half of all new navigation trainees were affected. If you were sick on more than three flights, your cadet days were ended. Fortunately I was able to work without nausea after only two flights.

There was a cadet club on the base where you could relax, get snacks, read, play cards, or visit with friends. About a week after I arrived at Hondo I was pleased to run into Al Buffington at this club. Al had been two years ahead of me in high school. His fiancee, Ruth Maxwell, and I had several high school classes together. Ruthie, a bright, vivacious and friendly girl, was also a good friend of Mickey. They were sorority sisters at Stanford. Al had been at Hondo for a couple of months and we enjoyed comparing notes on the program and talking about mutual friends from home. As we got better acquainted, I realized what an outstanding person he was. We didn't know then of the close friendship that would develop after the war. Our lives were to demonstrate some remarkably parallel paths in military, educational, career, and family patterns over the next decade.

Apart from the cadet club and base movie theater, there was little to do in our spare time in Hondo. The town itself had little to offer. During off hours, we often swam at the base swimming pool for relief from the heat. When we received weekends passes I sometimes went into San Antonio with Skee Salisbury and John Meredith, friends from the Pomona program. In the city's center nearly everybody on the streets was in the military. With four of the nation's largest air bases, including Kelly and Randolph Fields, San Antonio had the greatest concentration of air force personnel in the country. Large numbers of soldiers stationed at Fort Sam Houston swelled the military throng in town on weekends. We were able to visit the Alamo and soaked up the Mexican flavor of this noisy, active town. We usually had dinner at the Meger, an historic hotel near the Alamo. We visited some of the canteens and USO service centers. The ratio of women to men was so low that we usually ended up going to a movie and then heading back to Hondo.

Perhaps because there were so many servicemen around, the locals made us feel less welcome than we had in Southern California. An example was the poor transportation available to travel the forty-some miles between Hondo and San Antonio. We discovered that hitchhiking was not a viable alternative to the infrequent and overcrowded bus connection. Skee and I were educated on our first trip into San Antonio. When we stood by the highway and put our thumbs out, we were encouraged when a rickety old sedan pulled over almost immediately. It contained a couple of other cadets as passengers. The driver said, "Where y'all headed?" When we answered, "San Antone," he said, "That'll be five dollars each." We learned from the cadets in the car that this was local practice and the going rate. This scenario was replayed on the return trip. So we shelled out better than ten percent of our monthly pay for each round trip to the city. During my time in the area, I never received a free ride.

At the base we settled into a routine that had us flying two, sometimes three, missions per week. We spent the rest of our time in class and physical conditioning. The most exciting thing that happened at the base was a fire that burnt down our mess hall. By the last week in September I had completed thirteen missions with passing grades and was feeling more confident that I would complete the program.

On September 24, the Red Cross delivered a telegram informing me that Mother was at the Mayo Clinic in Minnesota for a cancer operation. It indicated that, in view of her critical condition, I should if possible come to Rochester.

My response to the news was a mixture of concerns: some for Mother and the possibility of her dying and some over the effect that leaving would have on my chances of completing the program. At that time, and throughout several more decades, many of my decisions gave great weight to how the action involved would affect my image or how others would perceive me. I believe I was less upset by Mother's condition than by the possibility that a furlough would diminish me in the eyes of those who decided my air force destiny. I didn't make my dilemma known to the Red Cross representative who went with me to headquarters to inform them of the situation. An emergency furlough was granted. I also learned that, if I stood by at the airstrip control area, I could obtain transportation on air force planes headed in the direction of Minnesota.

MOTHER'S OPERATION

It was necessary to check out a parachute in order to take advantage of the free flight. By early afternoon I found myself aboard an AT-7 bound for Little Rock, Arkansas, where I was able to get a ride aboard another plane to Scott Field in Illinois. From there I got aboard a commercial flight to Chicago and another to Rochester. I had to check the parachute as baggage on the commercial flights. FAA regulations forbid passengers to carry them aboard.

I arrived in Rochester the next morning and went by taxi to St. Mary's Hospital. The weather was bright and cool fall colors beginning to tinge many trees. It was quite a contrast to the hot and humid area from which I had come. The size and number of hospital and other medical buildings that comprised the Mayo Clinic complex were impressive. When I located and entered Mother's room, I found my half brother Ledyard who had arrived the night before. Mother was clearly apprehensive but in good spirits and pleased that her sons were with her. I shared her pleasure at seeing Ledge. It had been nearly eight years since the Hellroaring trip when we had last been together.

The operation was scheduled for the next morning. After spending an hour or so with Mother, Ledge and I went to see her surgeon, Dr. Benson. He told us she had colon cancer in the rectal area and was going to have a colostomy. This procedure involves removing the cancerous portion of the lower colon, closing the rectum, and fastening the remaining lower colon to an opening created in the abdomen. It was a high-risk, major operation which at that time had been successfully performed only at the Mayo Clinic and a few other medical centers. We gained the impression from Dr. Benson that life expectancy was generally short for those who survived the surgery.

Ledge and I used the times when Mother was not available for visiting to get reacquainted. Fourteen when I was born, he had seldom visited us in South Pasadena. As a teenager he was in boarding schools in the East and had spent a year abroad studying in Florence before entering MIT. There he majored in city planning and met and married Virginia who was an architecture major. This time in Minnesota provided us the first chance we had to talk as adults.

We strolled around downtown Rochester enjoying the parks, the clean and bright look of the place, the fall foliage, and the feel of autumn in the air. We stopped for coffee in the hotel coffee shop and bantered with the friendly waitress who served us. Most of our conversations related to Mother. We compared stories she had told us about her life. Ledge recounted his memories of her in Montana at Crag Eyrie and in Gloucester, Virginia. I told him of my times with her in Southern California. I became aware that we both held negative views of Mother and were in Rochester more out of a sense of duty than of affection or concern. During my teens I had become increasingly critical of Mother. She seemed better at dealing with strangers and acquaintances than with those close to her. From the time I was a small child, she often asked, "Do you love me?" I always answered, "Yes," to this test of my fidelity. I came to wonder why she never showed spontaneous warmth and affection of the kind that I received from my father, Ree, and other family members.

Ledge's bitterness seemed deeper than mine. His words reflected strong feelings: "Mother pretty much abandoned me after she and Father were divorced. She gave complete responsibility for my care and education to my father. I think your father, Jack, liked having me around but Mother made no effort to have me live with your family in California. Both my parents were more interested in their own lives than in mine. I was shunted off to relatives and sent away to a series of boarding schools."

When Ledge asked me how I felt about my parents' recent divorce, I said, "It was not a big surprise. They had never seemed close for as long I could remember." I added, "I was kind of surprised that Dad got married again so soon." Ledge said "You shouldn't blame Jack. Remember that Mother left him for four months every year and it's natural that he sought affection elsewhere. Your dad is a fine man and I feel sorry for him having to put up with Mother for all those years. "

I still puzzle over the reason she abandoned her sons. Perhaps she was afraid to assume custody because she lacked confidence. At the time of our Rochester conversations in 1944, neither Ledge nor I was capable of viewing Mother with much compassion and understanding. It seemed to us that she was an interesting and often likable woman who had displayed few of the maternal traits we observed in other mothers.

Ledge observed, "Maybe she patterned her mothering skills after those of her mother. Granny was a tough and critical woman. I remember one angry scene at Crag Eyrie. I saw her reduce Mother to tears in my presence over some behavior that she considered inappropriate. She scolded Mother as if she were a small child. It's hard to see how Mother could have much confidence in herself if that's the kind of verbal abuse she received as she was growing up."

The next morning Ledge and I spent several hours in a waiting room outside the surgery area. Dr. Benson emerged to tell us that the first and most critical operation had gone well and that Mother's vital signs and general condition were good. She would be able to see us later in the day. He said he expected to perform the second procedure in about five days. My reaction to this good news was an intense feeling of relief, joy, and sincere gratitude toward Dr. Benson. My eyes were full of tears. When I shared this surge of unexpected emotion with Ledge, it surprised me to find he had experienced a similar reaction. We concluded that she meant a great deal to us both in spite of our critical views of her.

Mother was sedated and in some discomfort when we visited her that evening. Again, she seemed very pleased that we were there and attempted to make humorous comments on her condition and surroundings. She dozed off and we sat with her for an hour or so before returning to the hotel. After we talked to Dr. Benson the next day, Ledge decided that it was safe to return to New Jersey where he had some important professional commitments. Since I had a two week emergency leave, I agreed to remain for the second operation. We visited with Mother and I went to the airport with Ledge. We agreed that we wouldn't let eight more years go by without getting together.

Over the next few days, Mother recovered her strength and we had some good visits together. Her outlook seemed amazingly positive in view of the major changes that the colostomy was to make in her life. She would have to give up horseback riding and many of the vigorous activities related to ranch life in Montana. She was in good physical and mental shape for the second operation, which also went well.

With several days left on my leave, I took the late night train down to Madison, Wisconsin for a weekend visit with Beni Reinhold. After completing the pre-meteorology program at Cal, he transferred into a cadet electronics program at Yale. In New Haven Beni, and most of the Cal pre-met transfers who had not majored in electrical engineering, washed out after a short time because of the highly technical nature of the classes. He was sent to an electronics school for enlisted men at Truax Field, outside of Madison. The visit also provided an opportunity to see Helen Bellinger, who had been attending the University of Wisconsin there for the past two years. It was good to see these old friends. We attended a football game between Wisconsin and Marquette. I returned to Rochester by train and spent a day with Mother, who was making a rapid recovery. I then used a combination of commercial airlines and aerial hitchhiking to return to Hondo.

The day I returned I found that my class was out flying. This meant I had missed three of the sequenced navigation missions that were basic to graduating as an aerial navigator. I continued to attend class sessions, and flew a couple of missions with my class. However, the need to make up the missed missions soon led to my reassignment to the class scheduled to graduate a month after ours. In November, I watched the ceremony at which my friends Skee Salisbury, John Meredith, and John Anderson, classmates since Pomona, received their wings and commissions. I went into San Antonio with them to celebrate and, with a mixture of envy and regret, bid them farewell as they left for crew training in B-24s.

LIEUTENANT CHURCH

The final weeks at Hondo went well. The missions were made up and I found that I enjoyed being a little ahead on class work. When it appeared that graduation on December 10 was certain I telephoned Mickey and Dad. He said that he would be coming to Texas on business and would like to attend the graduation. Knowing how much he valued his commission and military service, it did not surprise me that he was making the effort to be there. I was pleased to discover that I would receive a commission as a second lieutenant. For some reason the air force had begun the practice of making a sizable proportion of graduating navigators and bombardiers Flight Officers, a warrant officer grade, rather than granting them commissions. So it was a particularly proud moment for both of us when former Captain Church pinned the wings on his teenaged son, Lt. Church. When I look at the pictures of that youthful-looking officer, I see clearly why the expression "fly boy" was used during World War II.

My father and I had a brief weekend celebration and visit in San Antonio before he continued his business trip. I returned to Hondo. While awaiting transfer orders, I critiqued cadet flight missions. It seemed strange to hear the cadets calling me sir and paying serious attention to my comments. In about ten days, I received orders transferring me to the Fourth Air Force. After a leave extending over the holidays, I was to report to Lemoore Air Base in Central California for assignment to a B-24 crew.

The holiday leave was a great success. Mickey and I spent a lot of good time together. We went on several dates with George Hall and Bee Emmons and Lewie Simpson and Betty Curl. New Year's day found us at the Rose Bowl enjoying the wartime contest between USC and Tennessee.

Two days later, I took a bus up US 99 to Lemoore. It was a damp, cold, and drizzly day in the Central Valley when I arrived at the unmemorable way point. Within a couple of days our newly organized squadron of flight crews was aboard a troop train headed for Tonopah, Nevada.

The ride on the troop train was similar to several other such trips I made around the West during 1945. The old Pullman sleeping cars were shabby but comfortable. The trains spent a lot of time stopped on sidings to accommodate the war's heavy railroad traffic. We had comfortable berths for sleeping. Most of us spent our waking hours reading or playing cards. I applied the poker skills acquired as a child, usually profitably. Our train followed the Southern Pacific route over the Sierra Nevadas at Donner Pass to Sparks, east of Reno, Nevada. There the train remained in the rail yard overnight. The next morning our rail cars were shunted onto a branch line headed south. At Wabuska our train was coupled to a locomotive of the Tonopah & Goldfield Railroad.

All day long we crept across the high desert basins and mountains. Forty years earlier my father traveled this same route during the major mineral rush that began in Tonopah in 1900. For the last sixty miles it was apparent why the miners of my father's day said the initials T&G RR on the ancient locomotive's fuel carrier stood for Tug & Grunt. The train moved at such a slow pace up the gentle grade toward Tonopah that we took breaks from our card playing and walked along beside the moving train. It is quite possible that the young bride of Charley Metscher, the engineer, was at the controls of the old locomotive. His nephew Allen told me she often rode with him on the long slow run and spelled him at the throttle.

TONOPAH

Our first views of the town added to our earlier concerns about Tonopah's remote location. It was in a desolate draw between several small mountains. A few multi-storied stone and brick buildings and a dozen or so smaller frame buildings lined the main street. The large head frames and work buildings of several mines were nearby. Small houses and shacks dotted the hillsides. As our train pulled into the station we could see a light dusting of snow on the hills.

The air base itself lay about six miles east of town surrounded by more mountains. When we unloaded our gear from the buses that brought us to our quarters, the cold January wind reminded us that we were at 6,000 feet. We learned later that one of the first units to occupy the base in 1943 had erected a large sign in front of their tent headquarters that read:

HEADQUARTERS
23rd AIR DEPOT GROUP
CAMP FROSTY BALLS

The hard-nosed commanding officer soon ordered the removal of this apt reminder of the climate. Cold winter weather was only one of the reasons fighter pilots and bomber crews cursed the pork barrel efforts of Nevada's Senator Pat McCarran that had led to the inappropriate location of the air field. Strong winds, often dust laden; the high altitude of the runways; the proximity of higher mountains; and the use of old and difficult-to-maintain planes returned from combat—all contributed to one of the worst air base safety records in the US. Many fighter pilots and bomber crews were lost at this desolate site.

Like most new arrivals, I was unaware of the particular hazards involved at Tonopah. We assembled as a crew the next morning. We wanted to meet our fellow crew members and get to the business of learning about the B-24. All of us wanted to combine our newly developed skills

Our B-24 crew, Tonopah AAB, 1944.
L to R, Back Row: Kerns, Church, Vance, Wells, Concemi.
Front Row: Kermoyan, Hightower, Strzuck, Imperatore, Hudson.

into a successful bomber team. Among my sevice papers I found a list of the crew and my first impressions:

Lt. David W. Wells, Pilot—tall, friendly, dapper and self-assured, in his mid-twenties

Lt. Robert Vance, Copilot—big, affable, easy going, in early twenties

Lt. John L. Church, Navigator—serious, nervous, just turned 20

F/O Frank Concemi, Bombardier—short, heavy-set, extroverted, happy-go-lucky, about my age

T/Sgt. Clarence Strzock, Flight Engineer—quiet, competent, oldest
and most experienced crew member, in late twenties
Sgt. Alex Kermoyon, Radio Operator—tall, good looking, confident,
and outgoing, early twenties
Sgt. Joe Imperatore, Armorer-Gunner—small, quick, most knowl-
edgeable of the gunners, probably in mid twenties
Cpl. Oral Hightower, Sperry Ball Gunner—quiet, and serious, alert
Cpl. Everett Kerns, Waist Gunner—unassuming, didn't say much
Cpl. Jim Hudson, Tail Gunner—friendly, good looking, articulate.

I don't recall any survival situation since that time when I have felt more dependent on others and more responsible for them. I could not take these nine men casually—what they knew, thought, said, and did was very important. I believe that this feeling was shared for we lost little time in getting acquainted.

We went as a group to the flight line for an indoctrination tour. It was exciting to see the twin-tailed B-24 Liberators lined up along the taxiways with guns bristling from their turrets. Armorer crews were ferrying practice bombs to their open bomb bays. Our instructor showed us how to climb aboard one of the big planes. At last we got to see the inside of a B-24, designed by Consolidated to improve on the speed, range, and bomb load of Boeing's famous B-17 Flying Fortress. These two planes had shared the heavy bombing effort of the USAAF during the first two years of the war. The larger, longer-ranged Boeing B-29 Superfort had begun long range bombing of Japan six months before we arrived in Tonopah. This new generation of heavy bombers was to end the war sooner than we expected.

As we climbed up into our designated positions within the plane we could see how the designers had achieved the lightness that enabled the B-24 to fly faster, higher, and farther than the B-17. The unpressurized and unheated interior was stark, its structural framework exposed. It felt like

B-24 over Nevada, 1944.
Taken from waist gunner opening while flying in
formation. Navigator's position is just above the numeral six.

being in a long, narrow, sheet metal workshed.

Clearly, crew comfort was not a primary design objective. During our subsequent training missions we learned that at normal flight altitudes, often 20,000 feet and above, working conditions were tough. We wore several layers of clothing topped by fleece-lined leather pants, jackets, boots, helmets, and gloves to endure temperatures as low as minus 40F. Oxygen masks were required to function in the thin, chilled air. The ice that formed around the masks impeded seeing, breathing, and talking. The heavy gloves made it difficult to perform tasks requiring finger dexterity such as plotting, handling tools, adjusting controls and instruments, or firing guns. Those who removed their gloves often ended up with frostbite and a stay in the base hospital.

The training at Tonopah was excellent. Many of the instructors had flown these planes in combat and gave us practical and useful hints on how to perform our specialties. For ground training we usually split up into our specialties. The gunners trained in ground versions of the turrets and waist positions they manned aloft. Pilots, navigators, and bombardiers spent hours in simulators that seemed remarkable to me. The crew officers trained together in a trainer that created the conditions of a full bombing mission. Aircraft and bomb sight controls operated and instruments showed speed, direction, altitude, wind effect. Simulated radio aids for navigation were provided. This pre-video technical marvel even projected on surrounding screens the physical appearance of the ground and sky along the flight path and target area, including celestial bodies.

I found the flight training as exhilarating as anything I have ever done. Being one of ten men working together to operate this big war machine and its complex systems was like being on a football team with the added intensity of knowing that mistakes could be fatal. We had to learn to perform the jobs of other crew members to enable us to complete a mission in the event of crew casualties. Frank Concemi, the bombardier, and I had to be able to handle each other's specialty as well as man the nose turret. On many of our training missions we would be "attacked" by P-39s acting as enemy fighters. The turrets and other machine guns carried movie cameras that operated when we triggered the guns. We would attend post-mission movie sessions at which we learned whether or not we had "hit" the attacking fighters. Even more rousing were the low-level strafing runs over the desert target ranges when we fired live ammo at ground targets. To sit in the nose turret between the noisy staccato of twin 50 caliber machine guns as the desert terrain rushed towards you a few feet below was an unforgettable experience. We also fired at aerial and ground targets from the other turrets. The most unusual sensation was lying on my back in the Sperry Ball Turret that lowered down below the belly of the fuselage. With only a Plexiglas bubble around me, it was easy to imagine myself detached from the plane and flying through the air by myself. Like the nose turret, the Sperry Ball was particularly spine tingling on ground strafing runs.

As the weeks rolled by, we got to know the plane and each other pretty well. Sitting in the copilot's position and having Dave Wells, our pilot, talk us through a touch-and-go landing was the cross training that most of us enjoyed the most. To me it felt like controlling a truck or piece of heavy construction equipment down a straight and narrow downhill road. I concluded, however, that the air corps had made a good decision when they made me a navigator rather than a pilot. My coordination and dexterity seemed to be taxed even by such closely supervised landings.

Wartime Tonopah boomed with the influx of military personnel. The town was a frequent off-duty destination. Housing for the wives and children of permanent party and crews in training was sparse and dilapidated. Several of our crew housed their families in the old hotel in Goldfield, twenty miles south. When I was a child my father had told me many tales about Goldfield and other Nevada towns where he worked as a mining engineer. Tonopah, in 1945, seemed to consist mainly of bars, eating places, prostitution houses, and hotels, some of which increased their share of the military payroll with gambling. Ten years later my wife, looking through an old checkbook of mine, noted that during those five months I wrote a good number of checks to the Mizpah Club to pay for losses at the black-jack tables.

Those of us from Southern California found that our schedule at Tonopah permitted an occasional trip to the Los Angeles area. It required a long drive, usually at night, over mountain and desert roads. A group of us made the trip every couple of weeks in a car owned by one of the pilots on another crew. Sometimes we arrived back just before the 5:00 a.m. briefing sessions that preceded morning missions. It was fun to get home but I began to notice that I was becoming nervous about such drives and the stress that seemed to be building about the flight missions. We had become aware of Tonopah's poor safety record. I was increasingly apprehensive, particularly on flights when I had seen pilots up late and boozing at the officers' club only a few hours before our takeoffs.

On one night mission that took us over the San Bernardino area of Southern California, I was particularly tense. The visibility was poor and I was not certain that my dead reckoning plot had me in our precise position. We were flying at 10,000 ft. I knew that Mt. San Gorgonio, about 25 miles west of San Bernardino, was over 11,000. As I rechecked my plot and attempted to get a couple of radio bearings, I called the pilot on the inter-com and said, "Navigator to pilot." He answered, "Go ahead, John." I came back, "Dave, would you take us up to 12,000 thousand? I want to recheck our position." He responded, "Negative, the mission is cleared for this alti-tude." My response, in which I (and probably the listening crew) could hear my anxiety was, "Dave, please take her up. There are some mountains in the area higher than our present altitude." When he answered with a touch of anger in his voice, "Calm down, we're okay here. I know where we are"—I knew I had made a major blunder. I should not have indicated my uncertainty and concern over the intercom. The confidence I had built up, that I was filling my crew role effectively, took a real hit. A few minutes later, Dave asked me for a course and ETA to our next turning point which I was then able to give him. The rest of the mission went well. After we landed no one said anything about my exchange with Dave.

Although I berated myself for not being a calm and courageous airman, I continued to get good ground school and mission ratings. Shortly before we graduated, our squadron CO asked me to fly as navigator with a special crew. We were to search for and destroy an enemy submarine sighted off the California Coast. I felt honored to fly this search mission in which the other crew officers were combat veterans who outranked me by at least two grades. We carried live bombs and ammunition and spent about six hours flying an intricate but unsuccessful search pattern extending out about two hundred miles from the coast south of Monterey. After this exciting day, I returned to my crew to complete our training missions.

IDAHO

After graduation, members of our crew all received different assignments. I had expected to go overseas as B-24 crew member. Instead my orders sent me to Mountain Home AAFB in Idaho to receive further training to become navigator on a new bomber, the B-32. On the troop train to Mountain Home, I found that most of us had never even heard of the B-32. When we got to our new base we found no B-32s. We were to take ground school classes there in Idaho until our planes were completed at the Consolidated plant in Fort Worth, Texas. We settled in for what was to be a six week stay.

We did not train as crews but focused on our new plane from the viewpoint of our specialties. Consolidated had developed the B-32 Dominator as its answer to the B-29 Superfortress that was currently making headlines with its land-based raids on Japan. Consolidated's development effort had started a couple of years after Boeing's. By the time we arrived at Mountain Home only about thirty B-32s were in combat in the Pacific Theater. This was in marked contrast to over 12,000 B-24s built by Consolidated that had seen service in all parts of the world and to the hundreds of B-29 Superforts produced by Boeing in the preceding year. We would be manning a plane still in the experimental stage. Its appearance was quite different from the B-24. It had a sleek, round look with a single, large, high tail. Flight capabilities such as speed, range, altitude, and maximum bomb load were a close match with those of the B-29.

The only new navigation system I had to learn was Loran. By this method location was determined by measuring time differences between radio signals received from widely spaced ground transmitters. It involved peering into a hooded cathode ray tube and twiddling knobs to move and match representations of the radio signals. It was much like the video games of today with a similar kind of time pressure. The navigator had to manipulate the flickering images, interpret them, and plot quickly because the high speed of the aircraft could take us miles away from the calculated position each minute. It was a wonderful addition to the navigation process because it provided an additional means of determining where we were when visibility obscured the ground or overcast skies prevented celestial sightings. Decades later, I found this early Loran training useful when navigating sailboats equipped with simplified versions of the same system.

Since there were no bombers based at Mountain Home it was difficult for air crew members to get the minimum hours of flying time required each month to receive flight pay. The pilots were able to log time in the AT-6 fighter training planes that were on the base. Navigators and bombardiers could get their time by flying with them in these two-place trainers. The only difficulty from my standpoint was the fact that many bomber pilots would have preferred to be fighter pilots and took these flights as an opportunity to practice aerobatics. Some otherwise thoughtful and considerate pilots seemed to take particular pleasure in seeing if they could get their passengers airsick. Nevertheless, we flew some nice side trips to Spokane, and other nearby airfields and got another opportunity see some beautiful country. Some would let us fly the plane that was much more responsive than the B-24.

Soon after I arrived in Idaho I heard some shocking news. The remaining members of the car pool with whom I had regularly ridden between Tonopah and Los Angeles had all been killed in a high speed collision in the early morning hours on the highway between Bishop and Lone Pine. I was shaken and saddened. Perhaps this tragic event explained the sense of foreboding I had often felt during those long dark rides across the Nevada desert.

Except for a few hours of class each week day, I had plenty of time to explore my new location in southern Idaho. Mountain Home was as misnamed as Big Timber, Montana in that there was nothing in its surroundings to suggest the town's title. The lava flow that had created the Snake River Plain of the Columbia Plateau had left a table top flatness in the area where the air base was located. I verified how level the terrain was when I decided to hike over to fish in the Snake River, which a road map indicated was about two miles south of our quarters. As I set out in that direction across the level, scrubby desert terrain, I was puzzled that I could see no signs of the river between me and the distant horizon. I had been warned about rattlesnakes. I kept a wary eye out for them as I moved along at a good pace. After about a half hour, I began to wonder if I was headed in the wrong direction. All of a sudden I stopped short and caught my breath. I had nearly stepped over the edge of a sheer precipice dropping down several hundred feet. I looked across a gorge about a half mile wide with the river running through the valley floor far below. I saw that the top and vertical face of the cliffs on the other side exactly matched the level where I was standing. After looking around for a way down, I finally gave up my fishing plans and returned to the base. I had received a geology lesson that vividly illustrated the depth of the ancient lava flow that covered such a large part of Idaho, Oregon, and Nevada.

I made some friends among the other flying officers. Most weekends one or two of us would go by train or bus to Boise, Idaho's capital about 40 miles northwest, or to Twin Falls, a smaller town lying about 90 miles southeast. I preferred Twin Falls because it was a friendlier place, with far fewer military visitors. It was set in the middle of a beautiful agricultural area. The green and fertile fields received water brought there by the Carey Act water system so well fictionalized in Wallace Stegner's novel *Angle of Repose*. The town had a small USO service center which on Saturday nights sponsored dances held in a large hall near the middle of town. There were many girls about our age in attendance who were glad to have dance partners. Jack, a bombardier, and I became acquainted with several of these young women. They made us feel very welcome on subsequent visits by showing us around the town, inviting us into their homes, and taking us on picnics. They showed us some of the nearby attractions such as the magnificent Shoshone Falls on the Snake River.

Another girl, several years younger than these women, made a more lasting impression on one of our last visits to Twin Falls. Probably around fifteen, Nancy, a small, shapely, and energetic girl, seemed particularly smitten by the young flying officers who visited her small town. When I danced with her at the Saturday night dance I noticed that she danced closer and moved against me in a much sexier way than my previous dance partners. At the conclusion of our dance together, she snuggled up to me and asked where I was staying. When I told her that I was at the Perrine Hotel she said, "Why don't I meet you there so we can get better acquainted." I was surprised and tried not to show my amazement at this suggestion. Nancy was clearly below the so-called age of consent. I had heard plenty of barracks talk about the legal dangers involved with girls of her age, labeled "San Quentin Quail" by wary servicemen. I somewhat nervously declined her offer, mumbling something about having promised to meet Jack, and went to find him and the other girls.

Later that night, after the dance, I went back to my hotel room, still thinking about Nancy's offer. I undressed, got into bed, and had just turned out the light when there was a tapping on the door. I got up, pulled on my pants, and opened the door. There was Nancy, looking at me with a sly, pleased look on her face. She slipped past me into the room and pulled the door shut. "How did you find me?" I stammered, concerned that she had been seen entering my room. She smiled, "Didn't you see me in the lobby? I saw you pick up your key at the desk. Here I am." I could see that. My half-awake mind was gradually focusing on the situation. How could I get rid of her without hurting her feelings? Worse yet, how could I avoid making her angry enough to call for help, contact her parents, or alert others? I could visualize arrest and an appearance in court for statutory rape or contributing to the delinquency of a minor. This was not exactly how I had planned to end my military career.

I began with a few gently phrased questions. "Do your parents know where you are? Is there a time you're supposed be home? Aren't you kind of young to be up so late and visiting in a man's hotel room?" She looked at me with a trace of defiance and said, "My parents don't care where I am." And then more softly, "I'm not as young as you think. Let me show you." She crossed the room, sat on the edge of the bed, removed her shoes, and began to unbutton her blouse. It was becoming increasingly clear that she had a mature body and instincts. I was feeling shaky and uncertain of my resolve as I took her hand and said, "No, Nancy, you're pretty and it's hard to resist you, but I don't think it's right for you to be here. Let me walk you home. We can meet tomorrow morning and spend some time together. We should know each other better before giving in to how we feel right now." This stopped her. She looked very young and vulnerable as she buttoned her blouse and put on her shoes. After we got outside the hotel and had walked a couple of blocks, Nancy said she lived close by and wanted to go home alone. We agreed to meet at a local cafe in the morning and she walked quickly away. We had a friendly and subdued meal together the next morning. She told me about herself and I told her about what I had been doing, including my engagement to Mickey. It seemed to me that she looked at the previous evening as just another adventure in her active life. I never saw her again.

As I recall this incident of nearly fifty years ago, honesty compels a further observation. A reader might wrongly conclude that the outcome of the encounter was the result of compassionate and honorable attributes on my part. The truth is that, then as in later years, I harbored fantasies of such erotic opportunities. I believe that noble thoughts of moral rectitude had little influence on my behavior in that Twin Falls hotel room. My reaction stemmed from doubts about my sexual prowess coupled with a self-serving fear of legal and career consequences.

Final Weeks of the War

In July we received orders transferring us to Fort Worth Army Air Force Base. Again we traveled by troop train and a couple of days later I found myself back in hot and humid Texas. The base was located in a suburban area of lakes and wooded hills only a few miles from the center of town. We transferred our gear from the buses that brought us from the train station into long, narrow, single-storied quarters. From our rooms we could look across Lake Worth to the big Consolidated Aircraft plant. At last we got sight of our new planes, parked along the aprons of the big runways. Their streamlined contours and bright new aluminum surfaces looked good to us compared to the old combat-worn B-24s in which we had trained. We were even more pleased the next day when we saw the interiors of the planes. Pilots, bombardier, navigator, engineer, and radio operator all operated from a large and roomy flight deck area. It even had carpeting and sound and heat insulation.

We were given what were termed temporary crew assignments and attended our first briefing session. The colonel who addressed us indicated that our time in Fort Worth would be brief. There would be a short period of orientation and a few training missions in Texas, but the intent was for us to get most of our training en route and in the Pacific. He said this training approach had worked well for the B-29 crews. It had enabled the air force to deliver a tremendous bombing effort against Japan in a period of only a few months. In fact, a number of crews in our group had already departed for the Pacific.

The working conditions aboard the B-32 were certainly far superior to anything we had seen before and the new instruments and systems such as Loran made my job much easier. In addition to several training flights in the brand new planes, we spent quite a bit of time in class and in the excellent mission simulators that had been developed for the B-32. After a couple of weeks we were told that we would be departing for Guam in ten days. Surprisingly, we were given a week's home leave before our scheduled departure.

On Saturday, August 4, leave orders in hand, I checked with base air control and was able to catch a C-47 headed for Roswell, New Mexico. When I got to this desolate bombardier's training base, I found no planes heading for the West Coast. With no other transportation available, I decided to hitchhike. I took the base bus into town and lugged my B4 bag out to the westbound edge of US Highway 70. As it was not considered good practice for commissioned officers to beg rides, I removed the insignia from my khaki uniform and stuck out my thumb as Private Church. It worked and I soon got a ride as far as Alamogordo. Little did I know that our route had taken us close to where the world's first atomic bomb had exploded only two and half weeks earlier. Unaware of this momentous event or its effect on the world and my participation in the war, I continued my hot trek across the deserts of the Southwest. Through the kindness of a variety of interesting drivers, I arrived in Southern California late the next day.

Mickey was at Stanford during the summer to complete the final five units required for her degree. As soon-to-be Phi Beta Kappas, she and Ruthie Maxwell were breezing through a beginning German course. Ruthie agree to take class notes and phone Mickey the reading assignments, enabling her to return home to spend the week with me. We were grateful and happy to be together for what we expected would be our last time before I went overseas. Having no car, I usually walked the two miles from my dad's house on Wilson Avenue to her home. Very few friends were around. We went to a few movies but mostly spent our time together at her home or mine. On the second afternoon we were at her house, talking with her sister Barbara, when the music on the radio was interrupted by a spe-

Mickey and I celebrate the chance to be together in the spring of 1945

cial news bulletin. President Truman had just announced that a B-29 had dropped a new and powerful bomb on Hiroshima that had reportedly destroyed the entire city. The bomb was said to be the result of secret US atomic research and had released an instant burst of energy greater than anything ever created by man. During the next 24 hours, the newspapers and radio provided more details. The president had informed the Japanese government that other cities would be bombed with this devastating weapon unless Japan agreed to an immediate and unconditional surrender. I told Mickey, "It looks like I won't be going into combat. The war should be over soon."

Two days later, a second and more powerful bomb was dropped on Nagasaki with similar results. The day after that Japan agreed to surrender and we joined in the rejoicing and thanksgiving that took place around the world. I remember walking back to my house with Mickey on this first day of peace. The late afternoon sun was casting a golden glow on our faces. The flowers, trees, and other plantings in the neighborhoods we passed through had never seemed so beautiful. Our future now seemed more assured. Strolling along, holding hands, we savored the moment. We wondered how long I would spend in the service and what Mickey would be doing when she got out of school in a few weeks. She was considering a job at a brokerage firm in Los Angeles. We speculated on when I would return to complete college and on when we would marry. Life seemed to have treated us very well.

After this momentous and euphoric week, it was somewhat of a letdown to return to Fort Worth. There I found that Jack and several other friends in our squadron shared my mixed feelings about the recent news. It was a relief to know that I no longer faced possible death or disability from combat. However, feelings of duty and patriotism and all our training had prepared me for aerial warfare. Now I wasn't going to get a chance to do my part in the war. I felt then, and continued to feel in later years, some embarrassment or guilt in the company of friends and others who had survived the dangers and hardships of combat. We learned that our squadron's transfer to the Pacific had been put on hold while the Army Air Force developed its staffing plan for the period ahead. We were to continue to take classes and fly some training flights while such plans were developed.

It seemed unlikely that the B-32 would play any part in the occupation and winding down of the war effort. I guessed we would be released within a few months. I had taken the Stanford entrance exam at the same time Mickey had, during my junior year in high school. So I wrote to Stanford saying that I expected to be released by the end of the year. I requested entrance for the winter quarter, beginning in January, under the GI Bill. It had been enacted a year earlier to provide educational benefits for those who served during World War II. Our schedule was pretty relaxed for the next few weeks. I had plenty of time to complete the forms and to obtain and submit the transcripts and letters that Stanford requested. In early October I received the good news that Stanford had accepted me.

We used our spare time to get acquainted with Fort Worth. It was derisively known as "Cow Town" in Dallas, its larger and supposedly more sophisticated neighbor. We made several visits to "the Big D" to see the sights and watch college football games in the Cotton Bowl. I preferred the western feel and friendlier atmosphere of Fort Worth. We had some wonderful steak dinners in the grill of the old Blackstone Hotel, seated below several very large, polished, mounted horns of the famous Texas longhorn cattle. Some of us were invited to serve as escorts and dance partners for some of the members' daughters at a Colonial Country Club ball. It was easy to imagine how Rhett Butler had felt as I experienced for the first time the soft accents and flirtatious manners of attractive southern belles at the lavish event.

In the middle of October I received a copy of my demobilization orders, telling me to report to Davis Monthan Field in Tucson, Arizona for separation. There, where thousands of fighter planes and bombers were mothballed in the following years, I completed the two day processing required to return me to civilian life.

I believe my 34 months in the military provided a wonderful transition from dependence to independence and occurred at the best possible time in my life.

Chapter 9 College & Marriage

RETURN TO CIVILIAN LIFE

November and December 1945 were happy months in Southern California. An increasing number of ex-service men and women were returning home each week. The newspapers and newsreels were full of pictures of happy reunions with loved ones. Parts of olive drab, khaki, and navy blue uniforms appeared everywhere, worn in various combinations with civilian clothes. The Ruptured Duck emblem handed out at separation adorned many coat lapels. In South Pasadena, as all over the country, families and friends were getting together to trade war stories and welcome back returnees. In some ways many of us seemed to revert to roles played before entering the service. Sometimes tensions arose when parents and others who had remained home also reverted to earlier ways of dealing with those who had been away. Several of my friends voiced anger and resentment over being treated in ways that ignored hard-earned maturity, knowledge, and recent levels of responsibility. Dad and Marion seemed able to recognize the ways that I had grown and generously provided love, food, and shelter without attempting to control my activities or behavior.

Mickey was working for the stock brokerage house, Sutro & Co., in Los Angeles. We savored our chance to spend most of our evenings and weekends together and began to lay plans for the months ahead. Early summer seemed to be the best time for our wedding. I would try to find some work during the two months before I left for Stanford. She would continue to work at Sutro until I completed two quarters of study. This plan would give us time to earn some money and to find a place to live in the Palo Alto area. We needed the added funds to buy a car. When I first got back, we got around by using public transportation or occasionally borrowing one of our parents' cars.

I found employment with Railway Express at Union Station, the main railroad station in Los Angeles. It was a short commute on the Pacific Electric. There I worked as part of a crew of about ten who sorted and handled freight packages and luggage. Our covered work area lay south of the depot along a loading dock for trucks and cars. Overhead a motorized chain-and-pulley system pulled a continuous string of carts in a rectangular pattern back and forth through a sorting area between the railroad tracks and the dock. We worked at various points along this conveyer, referring to loading lists to remove designated items for local delivery, consolidate them, and assist in the loading of trucks. We also helped unload incoming trucks and sort and consolidate items for outgoing trains. It was hard physical labor but I was glad to find a job. It paid well and I enjoyed the humor and roughly expressed wisdom of the work crew. We had much fun even though the workload built up as the Christmas holidays approached. In those days a large proportion of Christmas packages went by Railway Express. The work provided a pleasant transition between the military and return to college—I felt none of the pressure I had experienced in flying and there were no problems to carry home at night.

Mickey and I went out more often as more and more friends returned from the service. Early in December we attended the wedding of Ruthie Maxwell and Al Buffington. They made a striking couple. Ruthie was vivacious and petite in a beautiful wedding gown. Al, who had returned from the Pacific only two weeks before, looked big and resplendent in his AAF uniform. Their delight in the occasion and their joy together made us wish we had set an earlier marriage date.

Most of my close friends who had been in the Air Force, like George Hall, Beni Reinhold, Art Krause, and Sandy McGilvray, were released from the service by Christmas. Using some of my savings, I bought a used Cushman motor scooter for local transportation. It was slow. I found it hard to balance and maneuver, but it beat walking. I shared it with George until he bought a 1940 Dodge a few weeks later. Mickey and I continued to borrow our parents' cars for dating and longer excursions. It was a time of celebration and planning for all of us. Nearly everyone was going to use the GI Bill to return to school. I was happy to discover that Sandy had also enrolled at Stanford for the winter quarter. We found we would be in the same living unit and made plans to be roommates. There were many parties during late December. The last major event of the holiday season was the Rose Bowl game. Several of us managed to gain admission from friends at the gates and watched Alabama trounce USC 34 to 14.

CAMPUS INVASION

When Sandy and I arrived at Stanford University a couple of days later its physical appearance was the same as I remembered from my several visits to Mickey during the war. We approached the campus from Palm Drive. The red tiled roofs of the big quadrangle of sandstone buildings glistened from the recent winter rain. These seasonal rains had washed the palms, eucalyptus, and other plantings. The grass in the fields and foothills was changing from gold to the brief period of green that marked each spring. The throng of registering students in the administration building made it clear that campus life was undergoing a major change. Stanford was not to revert to its prewar country club atmosphere. The majority of new registrants were returning veterans. We were the vanguard of GI Bill students who would increase the student body by nearly fifty percent during the next few years. Many of the arrivals were married. Most were older and generally more mature than the undergraduates they were joining.

During the next few quarters the differing interests and motivations of the veterans would affect classrooms and other aspects of campus activities.

Sandy and I were housed in Cleveland Hall, the old Theta Chi house on Alvarado just off the main row of fraternity houses. Stanford had given all the fraternity houses presidential names and used them as men's dorms during the war. We were happy to find that our friend Jack Croul was also assigned to Cleveland. Jack's laconic, friendly, and almost shy manner belied his military achievements. I know of no other member of our high school class who attained the rank of captain. Highly decorated, Jack had recently returned from an impressive and hazardous tour of duty over Europe. He had served as a lead navigator on the B-17 raids that had contributed so much to Germany's defeat. Both Sandy and Jack had great senses of humor and were always ready to join in any socializing or other campus adventures.

I was surprised to find how much I enjoyed being back in an academic setting. Stanford had recognized two years of college credit for the year I had spent at Pomona College and another six months' worth for the pre-flight and navigation training. I still needed to complete some freshman requirements such as History of Western Civilization and a couple of quarters of foreign language. Western Civ, as generations of Stanford students called it, turned out to be one of the best college courses I ever took. Rix Snyder, was an outstanding teacher. I liked the hours spent reading in the Western Civ library. Snyder's classroom presentations stirred an excitement I had never felt in the science and math courses that had comprised most of my college work up to that time. The brief views of the philosophers and religions that the course presented made me aware of the depth and diversity of human thought and beliefs. The colorful panorama of Middle Eastern and European history, particularly the Renaissance, kindled what would be a continuing interest in history and belief in our individual and collective potential.

I had not selected a major, but the nature of the credits I brought to Stanford seemed to be pointing toward engineering or science. During my first two quarters I took several engineering courses and the first course in geology. I made these selections in part because I felt the implied career choice would please my father. I did enjoy the geology field trips around the Bay Area. I also found the surveying course interesting. Like navigation it involved sighting and plotting. With transits and poles we trudged around one of the nearby hills surveyed by generations of Stanford engineering students. They had driven so many marker stakes into this hillside that it was often difficult to find a spot in which to hammer another. The wonderful peninsula climate made it great to be outdoors.

Sandy and I decided to go out for some athletic sport. Sandy had been on the track team in high school so we went to the initial meeting for the track squad. Because many former track team members were still in the service, there were only three men present with previous college track experience. My chief memory is of the talk Jack Weiershauser, the track coach, gave to the assembled hopefuls. In football and other sports at Stanford the main athletic target was Cal. It became apparent that Jack's focus was different. He said that his main goal for the team was to beat USC. He launched into a tirade against the Trojans, whose track team, coached by Dean Cromwell, had been number one nationally for many years. Looking around at the assembled group, it was hard to see how Jack could achieve his goal. What did become clear within a day or two of practice was that, even with my lower weight and better conditioning, I was not a serious candidate for any track event. I had not found any team candidate slower than I. In each of the field events there were better prospects than I. An example was Sandy, who threw the javelin well.

During the second week of track practice, I looked across the practice fields and saw a strange sort of gang mayhem. Men in shorts from opposing teams were forming into a big pushing huddle. From this shoving mass one of the teams extracted a football and began running, passing, and kicking the ball. The opposite team was attempting to intercept passes or tackle the man carrying the ball. When I asked what was going on, I was told they were practicing for rugby. I had heard of this traditional English sport but had never seen it played. It looked great to me, so I trotted over and talked to the man who appeared to be running the practice. He was Pete Kmetovic, a famous Stanford football player, who said this was one of the team's first practices and they were still looking for players. I lost no time getting back to Jack Weiershauser to tell him I was switching to rugby. He smiled, concurred that I had no future in track, and wished me well in my new sport.

The equipment check-out was simple. I traded in the track shoes for football shoes and received some shorts, a jersey, and some sweats. I found that most of the aspiring ruggers were football players attracted by the sport's resemblance to American football that had derived from it. As in the track practice, there were only a handful of men present who had played competitive rugby before. Kmetovic's approach was low-key and everyone seemed to enjoy the practices. It took a few days to master the rules and pattern of the game and to get in condition for the soccer-like continuity of running and contact. It seemed strange not to have shoulder pads for a sport that required tackling.

I found that I did pretty well at the game. During the first week of practice, I managed to extract the ball from a scrum. I broke away for a fairly long run before making a lateral pass to one of the half backs who continued the rush and kicked a goal. When we opened our season the following weekend against the Menlo Ramblers, I was surprised to find myself on the starting team, designated as "break away." Although we only won one game out of four in our brief season, it was as enjoyable as any sport I've ever played. The high point was our "Big Game" played against the University of California in its Memorial Stadium at Berkeley. As we took the field to start the game, a huge member of the Cal team, Hank Wright, greeted me warmly. Beginning with Oneonta Grammar School, Hank had been a few years behind me through all the grades in South Pasadena. Hank and his teammates beat us 11-3, but the game was well played by both teams and enjoyed by the small but enthusiastic crowd that attended.

A decade or so later Stanford sent me a letter saying that the Circle S that I received as rugby team member was transmuted into a Block S. This upgrading was applied to Circle S holders in many other so-called minor sports. This is one of the changes the athletic department enacted to attract stars in sports such as rugby, golf, water polo, and volley ball. Stanford men and women have since won many national championships in such sports.

As the weather got warmer, Lake Lagunita was full of water and the campus and surrounding countryside became greener and more beautiful. I recalled the wonderfully descriptive springtime letters I had received from Mickey during the previous years. I missed her and stayed in close touch by telephone and letters. I went south to see her during the break between winter and spring quarters. When I arrived, I found that she and her mother had done a lot of planning for our wedding. The date was set for July 16 at the chapel at Our Lady of Mercy, the Episcopal Church in San Gabriel. They were working on guest lists, reception plans, and wedding gown. The number of details they were considering was impressive. Like most grooms, I had focused on the outcome of the event rather than its execution. The businesslike way Mickey and her mother, Lenore, were handling the planning was daunting. I occasionally wondered how much voice I would have in decisions later on, but when we were together, it seemed unimportant.

Spring quarter passed quickly. Emboldened by my success in rugby, I showed up at spring football practice. The atmosphere was quite different from rugby. The coaching staff led by Marchie Schwartz was tough and businesslike. The presence of large, well-conditioned players indicated that more men had returned from the service and that some serious recruiting had occurred. My experience as a tackle meant little when most of the candidates for the position were several inches taller and outweighed me by forty or fifty pounds. It was fun and interesting getting to know some of the players and seeing the planning and training that went into developing a major college football team. I welcomed the chance to scrimmage against these better players and worked hard to get in condition for the contact involved. It was clear after a couple of weeks that varsity football was not for me. Phil Bengtson, the line coach who later coached in the NFL, was particularly intimidating. He had little patience with anything but high level performance. One afternoon when I hurt my ankle in scrimmage, the disgust with which he said, "Get him out of there," made me realize that I would never make the team. This revelation was not surprising or depressing. Things were going so well in my life that I was able to place football in better perspective. Classes were stimulating, I was getting involved in campus activities, and I was eagerly looking forward to my approaching marriage.

Unexpectedly I found myself in campus politics. Martin Anderson, whom I had met during track and football practice, came by to see me at Cleveland Hall. He was running for student body president and thought I should run for Men's Council, the judiciary branch of the student government. He said that if I would encourage other students I knew on campus to vote for him, he would promote my candidacy for Men's Council among his circle of acquaintances. I agreed and submitted my name for the ballot.

Since I knew only a few people, it seemed improbable that anything would come of this. When the election was held a few weeks later I was surprised at the results. Marty was elected as president of the student body. I had received more votes than other council candidates and would be chairman of Men's Council during the next school year. Talk about shirttail politics.

I found that the chief role of the council was to judge reported violations of the honor code and recommend disciplinary action such as probation or suspension. There were to be a number of times during the next year when I found this elected job difficult and stressful. The very sensitive cases of students accused of cheating on exams and papers required more time and attention than I had expected. It would be many decades before I realized just how self-damaging it can be to place oneself in the position of judging others.

As the end of the quarter approached, I began looking for a place for us to live in the Palo Alto area. There was a severe housing shortage for GI Bill veterans entering Stanford. The university had acquired buildings of the Dibble Military Hospital in nearby Menlo Park. The barracks-like structures were being converted into dormitories for single students and small apartments for married veterans. The new housing area was called Stanford Village and had a long list of applicants awaiting its construction. I placed our name on the list and scanned the ads for other possibilities. There were none that met our needs at a rent we could afford.

GETTING MARRIED

In early June I returned to Southern California. For the few weeks before the wedding I stayed with Dad and Marion. I was able to help with the final arrangements and Mickey and I had plenty of time to plan our move to Palo Alto. Although we had saved enough for a new car, transportation was still a problem. The reconverted auto plants in Detroit were just beginning to produce the new models. Most car dealers had a backlog of orders. Fortunately my dad had put my name in with a local Chevrolet dealer early in the year and we expected to take delivery within a few months. In the meantime, we continued to use the Pacific Electric, the motor scooter, or a borrowed car.

For most of my life I have looked younger than others my age. This was certainly true as I approached my nuptials during those early summer days in 1946. The day before the wedding I went to the florist to drop off a list of flower requirements. The next morning the florist visited the chapel with Mickey and her mother to deliver and place the flowers. He caused great merriment when he said to my bride-to-be, "Your kid brother came by with the list." Apparently my father also considered me more youthful than I felt; he nervously approached me later in the wedding day to ask if I had any questions about sex. This was the first time I had ever heard him mention the subject. How could he think I spent nearly three years in the military without gaining such knowledge? I solemnly assured him that I understood such matters. I thanked him for the condoms he gave me without mentioning to him that a gynecologist had fitted Mickey with a diaphragm.

I don't remember much about the ceremony and reception. Wedding photos still in my possession show George served as best man, with Beni Reinhold and Mickey's brother Dick as ushers. Mickey's maid of honor was her sister Barbara. One bridesmaid was Betty Crowe, a friend from Stanford, and the other was Dianne De Veau, a friend and classmate at both college and high school. Most of my local family and friends mentioned in these musings attended. Ree came down from Sacramento. Mother remained in Montana, probably because she didn't want to be there with my dad and Marion. My recollection is that there was a kind of theatrical feel to the ceremony. Mickey and I smiled to each other on cue as she came

Mickey and I cut our wedding cake. July 1946. Interested spectators are L to R George Hall, Dick Magee, Ruth Maxwell Buffington, and Marilyn Wagner Raymond.

down the aisle on her father's arm. We clearly enunciated and projected our vows. I think we focused more on conveying the image of a loving couple than we did on each other. Perhaps later developments color my recall, but I don't believe I was the director of that evening's performance.

George had generously agreed to swap his car for the motor scooter during our honeymoon. So, after a lively wedding reception, we departed in his Dodge, midst showers of rice and drunken advice. We headed for the Biltmore Hotel for the eagerly awaited night of conjugal bliss. Our destination reflected a jointly erroneous belief by my father and me that this sumptuous hostelry, built in 1923 on Pershing Square in downtown Los Angeles, was still one of LA's premier hotels. The lobby with its famous art collection, rich paneling, thick rugs, and potted palms was as I remembered. However, our room, while large, turned out to be rather shabby. One big drawback that hot July night was the lack of air conditioning. When the bellhop opened the windows as part of his routine, traffic sounds drifted in along with only slightly cooler air. A nervous new husband, I made no effort to find us cooler and quieter quarters. I overtipped the bellhop in my haste to be alone with my bride.

Mickey had selected a sheer nightgown from her carefully assembled trousseau. She looked absolutely smashing. As we held each other in bed, whatever doubts about getting married that I had harbored in the previous few months faded. It would be stirring to report that I fulfilled all my long held fantasies that night. Such was not the case. Mickey was loving, receptive, and very much at ease. In contrast, I was bumbling, with a shaky feeling in the pit of my stomach. The long-anticipated event was diminished by my expressing my passion too quickly. I was embarrassed and disappointed by my failure to arouse a matching response in my bride. Mickey recognized my feelings and assured me that she had enjoyed our lovemaking and knew that with more practice, things would get better. Looking for-

Left to Right: George Hall, best man, enjoying usher Beni Reinhold's comments to the groom and usher Dick Magee at our wedding reception, July 1946.

ward to that practice, I fell asleep feeling grateful and happy that we were finally married.

We arose early the next morning and enjoyed the new luxury of having breakfast in our hotel room. Then we retrieved the car from the Biltmore's garage and set out on the long drive to Lake Tahoe. It was a hot trip through the Mojave Desert. The pleasure of being together and the wonderful scenery of Red Rock Canyon and the magnificent eastern face of the Sierra's made us forget the heat. I had become very familiar with this drive up US 395 while stationed at Tonopah. Just as my father had when he showed me this route a decade earlier, I pointed out the sights along the way. I still believe this stretch of highway provides one of the most spectacular drives in the US.

We were tired from the long trip as we drove down the grade at the south end of Lake Tahoe. A few minutes later we checked into the small resort located on beautiful Emerald Bay. Our cottage was located in the tall pines close to the lake shore. For the next few days we had a wonderful time enjoying each other's company. We mostly relaxed, sat on the beach, took brief dips in the icy water, ate wonderful meals, and did the things for which honeymoons are best remembered. We also took several hikes.

The most memorable occurred the morning I said, "Today, I'm going to demonstrate the skills I learned in the Crazy Mountains of Montana. We can make our way off the beaten track to that high promontory. It's about two miles away and we should be able to see all of the lake from up there." Mickey didn't greet my proposed trek with enthusiasm but agreed to give it a try. Several hours later, scratched from underbrush and nursing bruises from the more-vertical-than-planned ascent up the face of the promontory, she was even less enthusiastic. The last hundred yards were particularly taxing. We looked for handholds and places to put our feet and pulled our weary selves upward. I encouraged her by saying, "I'll bet we're going to have a view that not many others have the stamina and mountaineering skills to enjoy." The inappropriate nature of my comment became apparent a moment later when a small boy peered over the edge a few feet above us and called out, "Mommy, Daddy! Come see the people climbing up this side." When we reached the top we found a cleared and railed view site with several picnic tables behind it. After resting awhile we made our way down the wide and gently sloping trail that led back to the lake shore. Mickey quietly opined that the outdoor skills she had gained in Girl Scouts were probably equivalent to mine.

George was particularly glad to see us when we returned to Southern California at the end of the week. He and his girl friend Millie (later his wife) had been using the motor scooter for dates. They were pleased to return to the comforts of automobile transportation. Fortunately we took delivery of a new 1946 Chevrolet coupe a few days later. The car shortage enabled the dealer to load it with all sorts of unnecessary equipment such as fog lights and a rear window wiper. He knew we couldn't turn down the car. It was a handsome vehicle. For some reason I can't fathom now, Mickey and I dubbed it "Rosie." This name may have reflected our general outlook and expectations rather than the car's color, two tones of blue.

MARRIED LIFE ON THE FARM

Through a Stanford classmate, Maralyn Arnett Porter, we learned of a vacant apartment in an old house in downtown Palo Alto. Maralyn and her husband Dave, graduates of our high school in South Pasadena, lived in one the four apartments in the building. Dave was also completing his college work under the GI Bill. We stopped by to see them. They introduced us to Miss Hamming, a stern and somewhat forbidding spinster from Holland, who owned the place. She didn't seem too welcoming but grudgingly agreed to show us the rear upstairs apartment that was available. It was small and somewhat shabby but it looked okay to us. The windows looked out across an eight foot driveway to the wall of a similar converted residence. We discovered later that if you climbed up on the toilet in the tiny bathroom and leaned out the high window, you could see a patch of sky. We were pleased when she agreed to rent it to us. We figured it would tide us over until we could get one of the roomier and less expensive units for married veterans at Stanford Village.

We both got jobs soon after we got to Palo Alto. Since it would only be a few weeks before school started, mine was temporary work as a day laborer on the maintenance crew at nearby Menlo Junior College. Mickey found an excellent position as psychometrist at the new test center that the Veteran's Administration had established on the Stanford campus. They were fortunate to get her. She was an honors major in psychology. Her training included the kind of test administration and interpretation required. When school started we were able to travel to the campus together and could meet easily when time permitted. We moved into a new apartment in Stanford Village a few months later and had the fun of decorating it with cheap and homemade furniture.

Many activities were available to us on campus. My time with the rugby and football teams led to my employment by the athletic department. I became a member of the campus police who ushered and maintained peace at athletic events. Al Buffington, Carl Brune, and other high school and college friends got similar student police jobs. This enabled our wives to use our student body passes at the football, basketball, and other sports events at which we worked. Mickey had the fun of attending with Ruth Buffington and Mary Lou Brune, who had been sorority sisters at Stanford as well as high school classmates. We also made new friends at the parties and other events sponsored by the fraternity I had joined during the spring I had spent at Stanford before our marriage.

My grades fell a bit during that first quarter as a married student. I continued to have some doubts about engineering as a career. My grades in non-engineering courses had been uniformly higher—I enjoyed the liberal arts more. Finally in early 1947, I faced a choice. I could either use my remaining two years of GI Bill eligibility to complete the work for an engineering degree or use the time to earn an MBA in the Graduate School of Business. I opted for the later since I had enough credits to graduate at large with a BA. Al Buffington, whom I admired greatly, had also applied for the MBA program. So we received our undergraduate degrees in June of 1947 and were accepted in the fall class at the business school.

That summer Mickey and I joined a group from the University of Houston that went by bus to Mexico City and flew from there to Guatemala. We took classes at the University of San Carlos in Guatemala City and made field trips into the countryside. Mickey's fluency in Spanish was a big help in becoming acquainted with this beautiful and then troubled country. We flew back in time for me to start my graduate work. Mickey resumed her job at the Veterans Testing Center. It was a good time in our lives. We were enjoying each other, our work, our friends, and our surroundings.

This seems to be an appropriate point to close out these tales of my early life. I was then about as grownup as I ever got. I have never outgrown the view of myself as the Pasadena Cowboy who combines traits gained from both city and ranch living.

Epilogue

Those whose perseverance or curiosity has brought them to this point deserve to learn something of what happened to the principal players in the half century or more since these events took place.

My father and Marion had a good life together. They obviously loved and appreciated each other. Her political viewpoint was even more conservative than his. They became great supporters of General Douglas Mac Arthur and often listened to a phonograph record of his speeches. During the McCarthy era, Marion spoke at meetings of luncheon clubs and other groups throughout Southern California. Her theme was always the same: the threat of a takeover of our institutions and government by communists in our midst. During one visit to their modest home in Pasadena, Mickey and I said we were glad the University of California system offered a lower cost means for our children to attend college. They warned us that our thinking was dangerously leftist.

My father continued to garden and work on the stamp collection started by my grandfather. About once a week he went into the Los Angeles Athletic Club to join his friends in the lunch time domino games they had played for many years. He and Marion made many auto trips throughout the West. After his death from a heart attack in 1959, she moved to San Francisco to be near her children and grandchildren. She died there about ten years later.

Mother lived much longer. She returned to Montana during World War II and lived there the rest of her life. She and Aunt Allie lived together in Bozeman and Livingston. After Allie died in 1947, Mother lived alone in Livingston for several years. She then returned to Sweet Grass County where she had spent most of her early life. She rented a small apartment in Big Timber and continued to visit the Lazy K Bar on an extended basis each summer. Several generations of guests and family at the dude ranch enjoyed her piano playing and recollections of early ranch life. Her colostomy made it difficult for her to participate in most of the outdoor activities. For several years in the 1960s Uncle Paul arranged for her to spend her summers at a beautiful ranch in Sweet Grass Canyon that he had acquired from the Brannans. No one else lived there except Riley, the old caretaker. This ranch's site in the Crazy Mountains is more pastoral than the rugged setting of the K Bar. Later, Spike's daughter Michelle, known as Shelley, and her husband Bill Carroccia took over the ranch. They raised cattle and established the Sweet Grass Ranch which they developed into a very popular guest ranch.

Mother usually visited Ledge and Virginia and their children at their homes in New Jersey and Michigan at least once a year. She made similar annual visits to Mickey and me and our family. After each visit, most of us, particularly her daughters-in-law, were pleased to see her return to Montana. She required more attention than we were able to give her. She upset the household by commenting on our lack of discipline and injecting herself into our dealings with our children. We enjoyed singing with her but found conversation difficult because of her sarcastic and negative manner. She retained the practice I remembered from my childhood of asking her sons and grandchildren if they loved her without stating such feelings toward us.

She was in her late eighties when her short-term memory failed to the degree that it was not safe for her to live alone. We moved her from her apartment to the Pioneer Nursing Home in Big Timber. I continued to visit her in Montana at least once a year. Many of her nieces, nephews, and other relatives living on ranches in the area dropped by to see her when they were in town. She enjoyed piano playing and singing for the other patients and her visitors. I have a video tape made two weeks before her death at age 96, in which she played the piano and sang with my wife and me for over an hour. She was the last in her generation to die. The large crowd of relatives and friends who attended her funeral attested to their affection and respect for one of the area's true pioneers. I was proud to be her son. In her later years, I came to realize my love for her and recognize how my life was enriched by the interests and perceptions she passed on to me.

Most of the friends mentioned in these memoirs are still living. I have seen or talked to most of them recently. Marilyn Wagner Raymond lives in Monrovia with her husband, Fred. They raised three daughters. Both Marilyn and Fred had successful and stimulating careers, she as a teacher and he as an executive. George Hall graduated from USC and married Millie. They lived in Ventura where George established a very successful casualty insurance business. They had one son. Millie became ill and remained an invalid for many years. After her death, George married his present wife, Pam. They live in a spacious Santa Barbara home and travel extensively. I still consider George my closest friend.

Beni Reinhold graduated from Stanford. He eventually became head of the oil tool company established by his father. He built it into one of the most important companies in the oil tool industry. He and his wife, Darlene, live in a beautiful home overlooking the Pacific in Laguna Nigel. We have visited there several times in recent years. Art Krause graduated from Pomona College and received his MBA in the class following mine at the Graduate School of Business at Stanford. His career included public relations assignments for a major oil company and more than twenty years of marketing and executive positions in the petroleum equipment division of a large conglomerate. He and his wife, Pat, divide their time between their mountain home in Park City, Utah and Sedona, Arizona. Ralph Wood and his wife, Barbara (Risty), graduated from Occidental College. They have been very successful in the restaurant business. They raised four children and have lived in Palos Verdes Estates for most of their years together. They recently celebrated their golden anniversary.

It's appropriate to combine the report on Mickey's and my early married years with that on the Al and Ruth Buffington's. There were remarkable parallels. Al and I both married our high school sweethearts. Both Al and I were navigators in the Air Force. All four of us graduated from Stanford. Al and I received our MBA degrees from Stanford. We both accepted employment at a famous soap company. We were both assigned to that firm's Long Beach factory. Our daughter Sally was born in 1950. Within a year, the Buffington's daughter Dale arrived. In 1952, our son, John, was born, followed shortly by their son, Lee. Finally, the 1955 birth of our youngest daughter, Eileen, matched that of their daughter Lynne.

The families were separated by my transfer to Cincinnati and Al's recall to the Air Force during the Korean War. When Al left the service he returned to the Long Beach factory for a brief stay before joining a major management consulting firm. He was so enthusiastic about this work that he suggested I apply there. I was accepted and we both worked out of the firm's Los Angeles office for the next few years. I transferred to the San Francisco office to become head of administrative activities for the West Coast offices. A couple of years later Al left consulting to become general manager of the nation's largest walnut cooperative, based in Stockton, California. He was to spend the rest of his business life there. He and Ruth enjoyed the many years they lived in Stockton, with their children and grandchildren nearby. We were saddened by Ruth's death in 1994.

I remained with the management consulting firm for ten years and served many client corporations throughout the US and Europe. I was a vice president in the firm when we moved to the East Coast. Upon my arrival at the New York office, the partner in charge told me he had not supported my transfer there. He fired me a couple of years later. I became assistant to the partners of a major investment banking firm in Wall Street. After six years, I left to become VP of administration for a medium-sized brokerage firm. I resigned two years later to accept the position of vice president of planning for a large investment banking firm. There, I was to become VP and treasurer and eventually a managing director, on the board and executive committee.

Mickey and I divorced in 1974. Our children were grown and we had gradually moved in separate directions. I remarried soon after to Frances Conover Gagney. I had met her at a weekend retreat program at Wainwright House in Rye, New York. Fran and I lived in Stamford, Connecticut until 1984. After my release from the investment banking firm, we moved to Maine. During this period I served as training consultant to the organization that provided computer services to the NY and American Stock Exchanges and the NASD. Fran and I moved to the San Francisco area in 1988 and have remained here since. I consider myself blessed to have found Fran. She is an outstanding woman and a wonderful wife. She brought a son and three daughters, Richard, Carolyn, Aileen, and Sarah, into our extended family. In the twenty-odd years since Fran and I married, our combined family has added nine endearing grandchildren. Fran and I delight in each other and each other's offspring. It's hard to see how our marriage could be more fulfilling.

Putting these memoirs together has helped me see how the events and influences of my childhood and youth affected my life. My father taught me how to approach problems in a systematic way and to outline solutions. This helped me not only in school but later in my business career. I have come to see that the most important thing he provided was love and support. Unfailingly affectionate, kind, and considerate to me, he conveyed the idea of responsibility and commitment. He was not a disciplinarian and never used corporal punishment. I don't recall being ordered to do my homework or other tasks. He did at times convey his disappointment with my school grades and behavior. As best I can remember, the main reason I worked hard in school and other jobs was to please him. By indicating that he could perform tasks better and had done better in school, he laid the groundwork for my being critical of myself throughout most of my life. Thus, though I worked hard, I never felt I really succeeded in any of the jobs I held. Because I loved and admired Papa, it never occurred to me to attribute my problems in self-esteem to him.

It has been tempting for most of my life to blame Mama for many of my negative traits that caused me difficulty. I have come to realize, however, that blame is a self-defeating misuse of emotional energy. Many of my actions and reactions have been similar to hers. My short fuse or quick temper, tendency to speak without considering the effect on others, strong need for recognition, and practice of bragging to impress others were probably patterned on what I saw in her. As I grew older and suffered the consequences of such traits, I reached several conclusions. Most important of all, I came to know I can change my behavior and how I perceive people. There is no reason to emulate the negative traits of anyone. I now view Mother in a more tolerant light. Putting these tales together has made me better recognize and appreciate her strengths, talents, and love for me.

I feel a loving bond with my parents and all the others who contributed to what I am convinced was a wonderful childhood. The bond reflects a shared spiritual base that I can tap to value and cherish those in my life at present. This belief makes me look forward with great anticipation to what may lie ahead.

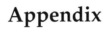

Appendix

*Mama holds horse by front porch of the Butte Ranch in 1901. What appears
to be a swimming costume was evidently appropriate ranch garb for the youngest of
the six Van Cleve children.*

Appendix A Mama and Her Family

The Butte Ranch

My mother was born at the Butte Ranch on New Year's Day, 1891, the thirty-fifth birthday of her father, Paul Ledyard Van Cleve. Named Charlotte Phillips, but always called Phyllis, she was the youngest of six children, five daughters and one son, born to her mother, Alice Mary Davis.

Paul Van Cleve and his wife Alice had moved West from Minneapolis in the early 1880s with their two eldest daughters, Agnes and Helen. The young family lived a short time in Billings, Montana. There Paul worked as telegrapher with the Northern Pacific Railroad, which was building a new rail line to the West Coast across Southern Montana. Later Grampy worked at the Northern Pacific stations at Big Timber and Bozeman, west of Billings. Two more daughters, Alice and Dorothy, were born in Billings during this period.

Paul left the railroad in 1887 to become a rancher. The young couple believed more money could be made in the cattle business. Through homesteading they acquired property on the lower slopes of Porcupine Butte. Their home site was near the small settlement of Melville, about 30 miles north of Big Timber. The area selected by the Van Cleves lay just to the east of the Crazy Mountains. Their new home provided a beautiful view of this magnificent outlying range of the Rockies. As one of the earliest settlers, my grandmother Van Cleve is one of those credited with naming the coun-

The Butte Ranch, home of the Paul Van Cleve family, in Sweet Grass County, Montana. Mama was born here January 1, 1891.

ty Sweet Grass for the distinctive, fragrant grass growing in the valley of the creek bearing the same name. Porcupine Butte rises several thousand feet higher than the surrounding foothills that level out to the East to become grassy plains stretching clear to the badlands of the Dakotas. Porcupine Butte received its name because it is shaped like a porcupine and the dark green stubble of forest on its higher slopes resembles quills. The lumbering critter for which it was named enjoys the salty taste of leather and is generally unwelcome. Ranchers must protect bridles, harnesses, and other gear from its gnawing teeth.

In this beautiful area of mountains, valleys, foothills, and range land lying north of the Yellowstone and east of the high peaks of the Crazies, you can see why Montana adopted the slogan Big Sky Country. The vast, ever-changing pattern of the sky provides an enormous and spectacular canopy over the area. Using craftsmen from the Norwegian settlement around Melville, the Van Cleves built a large, attractive, comfortable home from logs and locally milled lumber. They began a successful cattle and sheep raising operation. The child raising continued apace, with my Uncle Paul being born at the ranch in January 1889 and my mother arriving two years later.

I was privileged to know and remember all of the Van Cleve offspring, except Aunt Helen who died in 1901. An attractive, spirited group of women they were—plus Uncle Paul, a vigorous and forceful man who also plays a prominent role in my Montana memories.

Mother and most of her sisters never set foot inside a school as pupils. Their mother taught them at home and brought tutors to the ranch to supplement her efforts. Music lessons were provided for the older sisters. All of them that I knew were quick witted and displayed a wide range of knowledge and interests. I recall Mama saying that Aunt Agnes attended Juilliard or one of the other eastern music conservatories. Uncle Paul attended the one-room schoolhouse in Melville and spent one year, at age 16, at the Lawrenceville School in New Jersey, which his grandfather Van Cleve had attended.

MY GRANDPARENTS

My Montana grandparents differed from each other in many ways. I never really got to know my grandmother Alice Mary Davis Van Cleve for she died when I was four. She was by all accounts a charming, determined, and brilliant woman. Educated in New York at the Sacred Heart Academy, with some additional education in Paris, she reportedly spoke six languages fluently. She was an astute deal maker as well as an accomplished hostess and patron of the arts. Clippings and other family records indicate that she applied her active mind to many causes and projects, often related to the development of Montana. She frequently traveled East to promote her projects and causes, calling on businessmen, financial sources, and politicians to present her ideas. For example, I have, among the mementos from Mother, a photograph of Theodore Roosevelt. The president autographed it when Granny visited the White House accompanied by several of her children, including Mother.

My grandfather I remember clearly. He was a tall, courtly, quiet man who moved with dignity and grace. I don't recall ever seeing him outdoors when he wasn't wearing a suit coat with vest and tie. He had a mustache (the only one among my relatives) that felt bristly when he kissed me. His kind and sweet nature brought him a wide circle of friends and the affection and love of his children and grandchildren. He always found time to talk with young people. I recall his telling me stories about the Civil War period when his father's large family lived at Union army bases throughout the Midwest. He recalled the parades and military activity of troops being

Mama's Family Tree

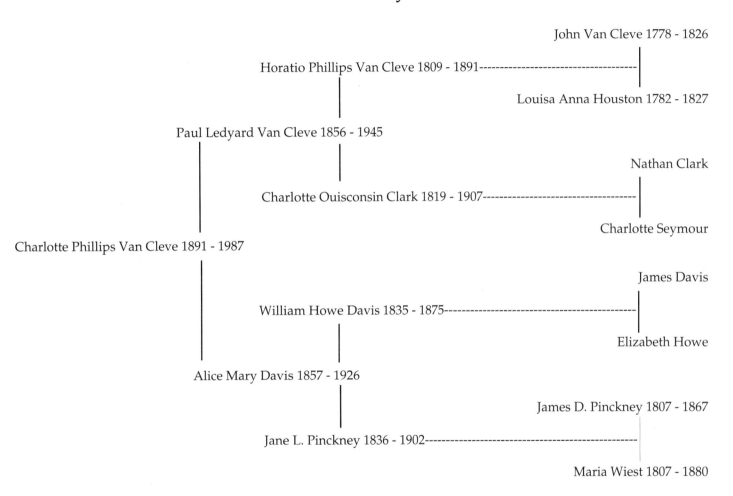

John Van Cleve 1778 - 1826

Horatio Phillips Van Cleve 1809 - 1891----------------------------------

Louisa Anna Houston 1782 - 1827

Paul Ledyard Van Cleve 1856 - 1945

Nathan Clark

Charlotte Ouisconsin Clark 1819 - 1907----------------------------------

Charlotte Seymour

Charlotte Phillips Van Cleve 1891 - 1987

James Davis

William Howe Davis 1835 - 1875----------------------------------

Elizabeth Howe

Alice Mary Davis 1857 - 1926

James D. Pinckney 1807 - 1867

Jane L. Pinckney 1836 - 1902----------------------------------

Maria Wiest 1807 - 1880

readied for combat. Grampy told me he served occasionally as a message boy and flag tender. His father, Horatio, a general in the Union Army, abetted his youthful participation.

The local Montana newspapers of the period carried interviews with Grampy quoting his theories of cattle raising. However, he seems to have deferred to Granny on most matters including the management of the ranch. He must have been overwhelmed by his active brood and particularly by his assertive and ambitious wife. One family source told me that at one point Grampy disappeared from the scene for a year or two; he was found living in seclusion up north near Havre and persuaded to return.

A free-spending woman, Granny apparently assumed that abundance would always be available to support her vision of affluence and cultural living for her family. Her efforts to fulfill her goals never ceased. As an example, my half brother Ledyard told me of her driving a team-drawn buggy overnight to Billings, nearly a hundred miles away, to close an important cattle deal. She still found time to write poetry and composed fifty-nine sonnets in honor of Queen Victoria, each depicting a year of her reign and each beautifully and intricately illuminated by hand. I recall seeing at the Monrovia home of my Aunt Agnes several framed copies of the warm letters of thanks she received from the queen.

My grandmother was a great believer in heredity and the abilities and advantages that she felt accrue from good lineage. She pointed out to her children her paternal ancestors, the Davis family, and her maternal forebears, the Pinckneys (with "of South Carolina" mentioned in the same breath), as examples. Mother wholeheartedly shared this view. She was equally proud of her Van Cleve lineage which the family traced back several centuries to Holland and England through her grandfather, General Horatio Phillips Van Cleve. His wife, my great grandmother Charlotte Ouisconsin Clark, was also an outstanding pioneer of the period. Her birth

Mama is shown feeding an orphaned lamb at the Butte Ranch in 1907.

at Fort Snelling in 1819 made her the first white child born in the area northwest of the Mississippi. The exploits of many of these colorful ancestors make absorbing reading. Mother always claimed she could tell whether one's ancestors were aristocrats or not by the size of that individual's hands and feet. According to her theory, small hands and feet were sure signs of nobility.

To return to Granny's marital goal for her daughters, each summer at the Butte Ranch found eligible young bachelors visiting from the East. She took her daughters to visit New York to extend their circle of friends. The success of this strategy will become apparent as we take a brief look at the lives of Mama's four sisters.

MOTHER'S SISTERS

Agnes Elizabeth, the oldest, developed her considerable talents and was reportedly the most like her mother. She became an accomplished pianist, both in classical and popular music. A bright and skilled conversationalist, Aunt Agnes was also an athletic outdoorswoman who was an excellent rider, polo player, and fisherwoman. I remember seeing cups she had won for sailing and golf.

In 1903 she married Bernard Beinecke Jr. of New York. His family owned the Sperry & Hutchinson Co., whose green trading stamps became an important part of the retail scene in the US. Agnes and Ben built a large home in Melville a few miles from the Butte Ranch and there had two daughters, Helen born in 1905 and Theodora born in 1908. Uncle Ben and Aunt Agnes and the girls moved to California around 1915 and lived in Monrovia near South Pasadena. My parents married at their home in 1923. Helen and Theo had sons about my age: Billy Schwartz and Tommy Burgess. As a youngster I played with them often. I recall the sorrow and shock felt in our home in the mid-1930's, when Uncle Ben, Aunt Agnes, and Helen all died from different causes within a one-year period. Theo became the bereft survivor of what had been a very close family.

The second daughter, Helen Pinckney, was, like her sisters, an active horsewoman and athlete. She enjoyed fox-hunt-like chases of wolves with hounds. When a wolf was brought to bay, she reportedly would ride in and club it with a long billiard cue butt she carried for the purpose. Such sport obviously reflected a prevailing frontier spirit quite different from today's sensibilities and urban concerns for the wolf's endangered status.

In 1901 she married a stereotypical British sportsman, John (Jack) Scarlett, of Gigha Argyllshire, Scotland. They built and moved into a spacious log structure that is still standing today not far from where the main ranch building was located. Her untimely death from diabetes at age twenty-three, after little more than a year of marriage, saddened the family. Jack, devastated by the loss, continued living at the ranch for many years after her death.

Alice, or Allie, was the most popular of all the girls and the aunt I remember best. She was a vivacious, friendly woman, with an attractive face and figure. Her striking appearance attracted attention wherever she went. She married Charles Horatio Dugro, son of Judge Phillip Dugro, of New York City, who had built the hotels Savoy and Saville in that city. Although they divorced within a few years, the young Dugros had one son, Harry, who was a playmate and youthful pal of my half brother Ledyard. Aunt Allie married several times and at various periods in her life was involved in operating ranches near Big Timber or Livingston, Montana.

Blessed with an optimistic outlook and a great sense of humor, Allie was fun to be around. During the last decade of her life, her hennaed hair seemed to get a brighter red each year. As mentioned earlier, she and

Harry were frequent visitors to our home in South Pasadena. She was very close to Mother and her death in 1946 brought a strong sense of loss to us all.

Dorothy Mary, the fourth daughter, was the only one who foiled her mother's plans to snare wealthy sons-in-law. Dora eloped with Jesse Langston, a poor but well-liked farmer from Georgia. Aunt Dora became a hard working Montana ranch wife, raised their five fun-loving children and took outside jobs periodically to make ends meet. She also had to learn to speak, read, and write again after a stroke in her mid-forties. In spite of such adversity she was a warm and friendly woman who undoubtedly had the happiest marriage of all the daughters. She and Jesse lived to celebrate their golden anniversary.

Uncle Paul

The family celebrated the arrival of Paul Van Cleve Jr. in 1889. As the only son, he received a great deal of attention and grew into a powerful and aggressive rancher. He inherited his mother's drive and ambition. Pictures taken of the family during the pre-World War I period show a much stronger physical likeness to his mother than to his father. Uncle Paul was raised to handle both the harsh realities of Montana ranching as well as the sophistication and culture of the East Coast.

However, he shared with most Montanans of his age the belief that the personal strengths and abilities required to live and work effectively in his rugged frontier environment were superior to those required of "dudes" who were raised and worked in less demanding urban settings. His educational exposure to the East was cut short when cattle revenues dropped and depleted family resources forced his return from prep school to begin his ranching career.

My mother, who worshipped him, had a fund of stories about his besting others in various tests of physical prowess or outwitting hapless Easterners. She described his freeing the victim of a wagon accident by lying under the heavy vehicle and lifting it by himself. Others may think of John Wayne as a perfect model of the rugged western cowboy, but I'll always think of Uncle Paul.

In 1910, he married Helen Perry, daughter of a prominent family from Montana's capital city, Helena. Aunt Helen was a graceful woman whose dignity and bearing were supplemented by energy and resolve. With her help, Paul Jr. began to develop a nice ranch on Billy Creek a few miles from the Butte Ranch. Uncle Paul delivered their first child, Paul L. Van Cleve III, later known as Spike, at the Butte Ranch in 1912, during a raging storm that delayed the arrival of the doctor. Charlotte Alice, known to the family as Dee, was born at their Billy Creek ranch in 1915. My grandparents' financial situation began to deteriorate due to market and weather induced problems in the cattle business. Uncle Paul pledged his ranch and other assets in a vain attempt to save their Butte property. In spite of his efforts, the Butte ranch where the senior Van Cleves had lived for thirty-six years had to be sold. Uncle Paul and Aunt Helen also lost their ranch to creditors and moved with Spike, Dee, Grampy, and Granny to a smaller, less developed ranch at Otter Creek.

Uncle Paul then began a vigorous effort to work himself and his family out of the mountain of debt that had been incurred. Through a series of shrewd and aggressive financial and land deals, he paid off the debt and began to amass a spread that grew over the years to thirty-two sections (square miles). Not all of these deals were friendly, leaving some neighbors and relatives feeling inadequately compensated for their contributions to the Van Cleve empire.

During his aggressive efforts to save and expand his family's land during the tough cattle years of the 1920s Uncle Paul gained the enmity of some of the neighboring ranchers. Shortly after the Butte Ranch had to be sold, Uncle Paul was arrested for threatening representatives of its new owners with a gun. They had challenged him as he removed what he considered family belongings from some of the buildings on the property. Later, in 1925, Sheriff Brannan, whose family property also adjoined the Van Cleves', brought Uncle Paul into court charging him with the theft of several cattle from one of his other neighbors. A few of his prominent neighbors testified against him. The list of defense witnesses included many Van Cleve relatives or their spouses. He was acquitted when the split jury could not agree on a verdict.

It was the founding of their dude ranch that eventually enabled Paul and Helen to recover from the hard times in cattle raising.

MOTHER'S TURN

In common with her colorful sisters and brother, Mama led a varied and noteworthy life. Phyllis was an attractive and energetic youngster. During an active childhood spent trying to keep up with her vigorous brother and sisters, she developed a unique set of social and physical skills. She quickly grasped and understood complex information or situations. When she chose to, she could fit in and communicate well with people in all walks of life. Sometimes her quick anger or sarcasm undid her ability to make friends and sustain relationships. In spite of her consummate skill in riding and shooting and her admiration of courage and western grit, her fearful side led to unnecessary stress for her and, as I experienced, an over-protective manner with her offspring.

By the time Phyllis arrived, her mother had perfected her child-rearing and son-in-law recruiting methods. Although given some extra freedom as

This portrait of mother filled nearly a full page at the front of the rotogravure section of the Sunday New York Times in late 1908. It announced her engagement to Thomas Greenleaf Blakeman. The editor's choice of this photo most probably reflected not only the stylish elegance of the seventeen-year-old subject but also the effective promotional activities of an ambitious mother from Melville, Montana.

the youngest, Mama was closely supervised and disciplined, particularly as to obedience and respect of elders. From her mother and other tutors she developed a broad range of knowledge and love of reading. She accompanied her mother east as a teenager and was introduced to the circle of well-placed friends that Granny had cultivated.

When she was seventeen Mama became engaged to Thomas Greenleaf Blakeman. Young Blakeman, an artist and sportsman, perfectly matched my grandmother's specifications for an ideal son-in-law. His family had gained its wealth and social prominence from the invention of the Spencer pen tip and the founding of the American Book Company. Mother and Tom Blakeman were married March 11, 1909, at the Butte Ranch. Reverend Pritchard of the Episcopal Church in Big Timber officiated. Granny had converted to Catholicism during her education at Sacred Heart Academy. Her first five children were raised as Catholics. In a rare display of assertiveness, Grampy had insisted that at least one of the children be raised in his denomination. Mother, designated as the token Protestant, had been christened as an Episcopalian.

CRAG EYRIE

The site of their impressive home on the southern slope rising up to Porcupine Butte provided an even more dramatic view of the Crazies than her parents' place. The large stone wall constructed to exclude grazing livestock still exists today as evidence of the home's commanding splendor. It was furnished with fine furniture, oriental rugs, and Tiffany lamps bought in shopping expeditions in New York. It was the scene of many big parties which often lasted through the night.

My half brother, Thomas Ledyard Blakeman, was born at the Butte Ranch on Christmas Eve, 1909. I have often thought that his date of birth

My father took this picture of revelers on the wall of Crag Eyrie at dawn after one of the Blakeman's costume parties. 1913.

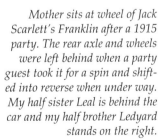

Mother sits at wheel of Jack Scarlett's Franklin after a 1915 party. The rear axle and wheels were left behind when a party guest took it for a spin and shifted into reverse when under way. My half sister Leal is behind the car and my half brother Ledyard stands on the right.

and mine, which also fell within a few days of New Year, reflected calendar sensitive attempts to duplicate the shared birthday of Mother and her father. I can visualize Granny contacting her eighteen-year-old daughter a few weeks after her marriage and saying, "Now, Phyllis."

YOUNG TRAVELERS

Tom and Phyllis divided their time between Crag Eyrie and Gloucester County, Virginia where Tom's mother resided at Neustead, the mansion of the Tabbs, an old Virginia family. Financial difficulties stemming from the Civil War had made it necessary for the Tabbs to share their home with Mrs. Blakeman. Bay Tabb, an older and partially blind member of the family, was nursemaid for my half brother Ledge. Bay Tabb's daughter, Margaret, became and remained Mother's closest friend.

As earlier counterparts of what would later be called jet setters, the young couple traveled to England in 1911 and 1912, bringing horses with them for fox hunting. They crossed the Channel to France for a few weeks each spring. They visited friends in New York and Connecticut as part of such annual travels before returning to Montana for the summer, fall, and holiday season.

Mother stayed at Crag Eyrie during 1913. In May of that year she gave birth to a daughter, who was named Phyllis Leal Blakeman. Leal, as she was called, was a round faced, beautiful child whose happy temperament brought much joy to the family. Photos of family activities during those years show that she and her brother Ledge were a part of most gatherings and events at Crag Eyrie. Sadly, Leal was only with the family a short time before her death from colitis two months short of her third birthday in 1916. Mother was devastated by her loss. I remember several occasions, years later during my childhood, when the memory of her daughter brought tears to her eyes.

This tragedy and the developing war in Europe appear to have changed the lives of the young family. My brother Ledge spent more time in the care of the Tabb family in Gloucester and the travels of his parents as a couple were curtailed. In 1917, Mother made a six-week visit to Hawaii to visit her father's cousins, the Halls. In describing this trip to me in later years she said it was made to soften the impact of Leal's death. She returned with memories of her island relatives' kind hospitality and vivid recollections of the beauty and unique nature of life in Hawaii at that time.

WARTIME SERVICE

The couple spent most of 1918 in Virginia. Tom Blakeman had enlisted in the military and was training as a pilot at Langley Field. Mother and her friend, Margaret Tabb, volunteered as nurses' aides at the military hospital at Camp Humphries, Virginia, and continued in this activity after Blakeman went overseas. Among Mother's papers I found a letter commending her for this volunteer service.

In early 1919, a few month's after the armistice that concluded World War I, Mother and Margaret Tabb volunteered to go to France. The YMCA had opened a number of canteens for the military personnel stationed there, awaiting return to the US. Mother, Margaret, and other American women served coffee and snacks and provided musical entertainment and friendly feminine conversation in these canteens. They received an enthusiastic welcome from the lonely doughboys. Many of the songs that we later sang with mother at the piano came from that period of her life. I still have a book called *Songs My Mother Never Taught Me,* which contains many of these World War I songs that she did teach me.

BLAKEMAN MARRIAGE ENDS

Tom Blakeman and Mother came back from France about the same time in late 1919, both with memories of successful service to their country. He was a decorated veteran of aerial combat and she a caregiver in hospitals and canteens. They retrieved my brother Ledyard from his wartime stay with the Tabbs in Gloucester, Virginia, and returned to Crag Eyrie and the influence of the Van Cleve family.

They only remained together as a family for a year or two. Clearly, they were unable to reestablish their relationship with each other. I am not sure why their marriage ended. Mother said later that Tom's proclivity toward drinking and what was known then as the sporting life made it impossible to continue living together. I am inclined to take a more balanced view and attribute some of their difficulties to Mother's temperament. She had strong ties to Montana, as opposed to Blakeman's interests which centered on the East Coast in Virginia and New York. She was temperamental and when upset could have a cutting tongue. I can't see her trying to reconcile any conflicts between them.

The Blakemans divorced in 1921, and Mother continued to live at Crag Eyrie. Ledge was sent off to boarding school in the East and returned to Montana for visits in the summer and holidays. I believe he spent more time in Virginia from that time on than he did in Montana.

HOLLYWOOD

After the divorce, Mother traveled to California and visited her sister Agnes who was living in Monrovia with her husband, Ben Beinecke, and their two daughters. During this period Mother worked as a stunt rider in the rapidly growing movie industry in Southern California. I think this was the only time she was employed during her entire life.

She was proud of her time in Hollywood and often described riding horses down cliffs and performing other feats that used the skills she learned as a girl in Montana. She enjoyed the glamour and excitement of film making and the chance to see and work with the stars and celebrities involved. I have a 35 mm film clip of a scene in which she and another rider swim their horses into a large river, lose their mounts, and are rescued by a boat. Although the scene concluded with a printed board with the notation *SAM WOOD* and a number, I haven't been able to identify the movie involved.

This brings us to the point where she got together with my dad, whom she had known in Montana.

Mary Letchworth Patterson, my father's mother, in 1881, shortly before her wedding to my grandfather Bradford Clifford Church.

Appendix B
Papa and His Family

Sterling, Illinois, where my father was born lies about 100 miles west of Chicago. His parents, Bradford Clifford Church and Mary Patterson, married in 1883. Papa's grandfather, Bradford Crane Church, and Mary's uncle, Samuel Patterson, both active businessmen, were partners in the milling firm Church & Patterson. Bradford Crane, born in Portageville, NY, had moved to the Midwest in mid-century. He had, among his other achievements, served two terms as mayor of Sterling. Following his death in 1883, my grandfather, still in his twenties, took over the milling business.

Some Earlier Relatives

As with Mother's ancestors, it has been fun to identify colorful contributors to my genes from Papa's side. I wonder if the way I go through life reflects the varied traits and personalities of these Church forebears. Bradford Crane's father was Lyman Church, who ran a store in Portageville, New York, where his teenage son Bradford worked before leaving for the Midwest. Young Bradford worked in retailing jobs around Chicago before marrying Mary Clifford. They moved to Kankakee, Illinois, where he established a hardware business. In 1860, my grandfather, Bradford Clifford Church, was born, the first of six children. The young family moved to Sterling a few years later.

Portageville is located in the scenic Gennessee Valley of northwestern

Papa's Family Tree

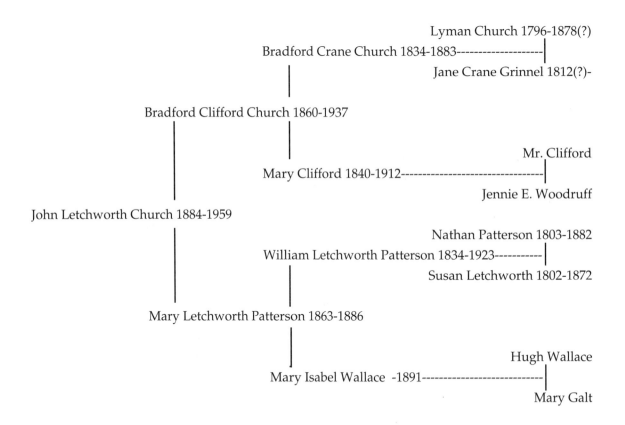

Lyman Church 1796-1878(?)

Bradford Crane Church 1834-1883--------------------|

Jane Crane Grinnel 1812(?)-

Bradford Clifford Church 1860-1937

Mr. Clifford

Mary Clifford 1840-1912-------------------------------|

Jennie E. Woodruff

John Letchworth Church 1884-1959

Nathan Patterson 1803-1882

William Letchworth Patterson 1834-1923-----------|

Susan Letchworth 1802-1872

Mary Letchworth Patterson 1863-1886

Hugh Wallace

Mary Isabel Wallace -1891----------------------------|

Mary Galt

New York. Both of my paternal grandparents had roots in this beautiful area. My middle name, Letchworth, which my friends have on occasion shortened to Letch, traces from Susan Letchworth (1802–1872), Mary's grandmother. Letchworth State Park, named after Susan's nephew, William Pryor Letchworth, immortalizes the name in upstate New York.

I have a book compiled by the Letchworth family. It extends the genealogy of that family back several more generations through Susan's father, William. As an infant he immigrated to the colonies with his parents, John Letchworth and Diana Webb, in 1762. From the same source, it is also possible to trace my Patterson ancestors back a few more generations.

Identifying earlier generations on the Church side has been less successful. I recall a conversation I had with an English friend who told me with great good humor that I would run into a dead end in such a search. He said churches often applied the name Church to illegitimate children left in their care. There is, nevertheless, quite a body of information about early families named Church in western upstate New York. Through the efforts of a distant cousin in Tennessee, I was able recently to determine how Lyman Church tied to earlier generations.

A Sad Beginning

A tragedy befell Bradford Clifford's young family when my father was 18 months old. The archaic prose of a yellowed clipping from the Sterling newspaper of February 17, 1886, his mother's twenty-third birthday, describes it:

> "Sad is the office of him who is called upon to announce the death of any young person. It will never appear just that one should die before age has brought waste of body and desire to depart. It is peculiarly so when as in the case of Mary Patterson

Church a happy family is broken up, two little ones left motherless and a large circle of
relatives and friends bowed down with the
weight of their sore affliction. It is scarcely
three years since B.C. Church, Jr. and Mary
Patterson were joined in holy marriage.
They had known each other from earliest
childhood and their affection each for the
other was as marked as it was fitting.

All this is ended, and the bereaved husband has but memory left to him—memory
of a wife always amiable, always loving,
always gentle. It was a most happy home;
she was happy in her worthy husband, in
her fine boy, (and latterly in her infant
babe), in her relatives and friends and the
happiness she felt she imparted to her husband and those who were of the circle of her
friends. . . . All that medical skill and the
most careful nursing could do were
employed to make comfortable her last illness and in effort to spare her life to family
and friends. Despite their best efforts she
quietly passed away early this morning."

Unfortunately the infant mentioned in this poignant obituary, my
father's sister, also died a few months later. Several years later, Bradford
married Edith Harden who was a loving wife and stepmother. So, in spite
of a sad beginning, my father was to have a happy and full childhood.

DULUTH YEARS

Although still in his twenties, my grandfather Bradford Clifford Church
was rising in the business world. He moved his family to Duluth,
Minnesota. There he combined money received from the sale of the Sterling
mill with that of several investors to form the Duluth Imperial Mill
Company. The new company built one of the country's largest flour mills in

Duluth. Its strategic location at the westernmost port on the Great Lakes and a successful advertising program contributed to the early success of the new company and its Imperial Flour brand.

My father spent most of his childhood in Duluth and nearby Superior, Wisconsin, where the family built a summer retreat. He learned to love outdoor activities, admire the wonders of nature, and meet the challenges of rugged weather. He grew into a tall, muscular, youth who participated enthusiastically in family activities. Photographs of the period show excursions, picnics, and many get-togethers with relatives and friends.

My grandfather left photo albums and scrapbooks filled with snapshots and detailed memorabilia such as passes, tickets, programs, menus, and newspaper clippings that wonderfully evoke the period from 1890 to 1920. These mementos indicate that my grandfather and Edith thoroughly enjoyed life and the fruits of his business success.

Shortly before the turn of the century, publications of the period carried stories of the efforts of international investors to form a combine of the major milling companies in the US. The Duluth newspaper featured stories of my grandfather's trips to New York where he met in Wall Street with the investment groups who were seeking to gain control of US flour milling and marketing. Several large independent millers like my grandfather felt that they lacked the resources to hold out in the face of threatened price cutting. He sold his company to the combine, to the dismay of his workers and the farmers whose wheat had been milled at Duluth.

ASOTIN

After a short period of inactivity, Bradford decided to move west to Asotin, Washington. It was a small community on the Snake River which there forms the border between Washington and Idaho. He bought a small

Four generations are shown in this 1895 portrait.of Bradford Clifford Church and his family. L to R: Bradford; his son, John Letchworth Church(Papa); his grandmother, Jennie E. Woodruff; and mother, Mary Clifford

My grandfather and father hoist and admire large sturgeon caught in the Snake River behind their home in Asotin, Washington, 1900.

flour mill and the family settled into a home whose rural setting was quite different from Duluth. My father was enrolled in the public high school in Spokane, about a hundred miles north. During the school year he lived with a family there and came home to Asotin on weekends and holidays.

My father enjoyed telling me about his time in Asotin. Two of his recollections impressed me. One was his description of the pet bear, which they raised from a cub. It was a case of a cuddly little playmate growing into a large, grouchy, unmanageable, and finally dangerous member of the family. The family had to return the adult bear to the wilds. Another concerned sturgeon fishing in the Snake River behind their house. My dad used a length of sash cord as fishing line. On one end he fastened a large hook baited with river eels. Papa would tie the other end to a tree and throw this sporting combination into the river. He hauled in some very large specimens of this prehistoric fish, usually after an overnight wait.

My grandfather apparently found bear raising and river fishing less fulfilling. He wrote Minnesota friends and former business associates that living in Asotin and running a small rural flour mill lacked sufficient challenge and excitement. So in 1901, after a year and a half spent modernizing the mill, he sold it back to its original owner and moved back to Duluth. He formed the Church Land Company, which specialized in buying and selling farm land. The family was happy to return to Duluth. My dad graduated from high school there a couple of years later.

MICHIGAN COLLEGE OF MINES

Papa chose engineering as a career. He selected Michigan College of Mines, 150 miles from Duluth on Michigan's mineral rich Upper Peninsula. I think Papa decided upon mining because of the public excitement and attention that gold, silver, and other rushes evoked at that time. Many working mines nearby enabled MCM students to gain practical work experience. Time in the mines supplemented what my father described as a very tough academic program of classroom and laboratory study.

There were many field trips to mines and excursions to various geologically interesting places. When Papa attended MCM, which later changed its

Many students lived in boardinghouses. The principal athletic program at MCM was the boardinghouse hockey league. The McCormick team, shown here with with my dad at the left, won the championship in 1905.

name to Michigan Tech, it was a small, austere, no-nonsense school. According to my father, it was highly regarded nationally. Its enrollment then was a few hundred students. It now has a student body of several thousand. When in later years I commented upon the effort required by my college work, my father conveyed to me his strong opinion that his courses had been much more difficult and demanding.

There were extracurricular pleasures in addition to hockey. He often enjoyed the company of a comely young woman, Jane Pryor. They sometimes joined other couples on picnics and excursions in the countryside. The many pictures of Jane, and their captions, indicate a smitten photographer. A common thread ran through the pictures taken in my father's

In Papa's photo album covering his college years this photo of a solemn Jane Pryor canoeing on the Pilgrim River. is captioned "Can't you see I'm lonely." Near Houghton, Michigan, 1905.

many years of bachelorhood. Most of them included beautiful women—even in some of the most remote areas to which he traveled as a mining engineer.

He graduated with the degree of engineer in "aught five," as he referred to the date. After graduation he continued to work at Michigan Smelter, which ran a large copper smelter in the Houghton area. He had worked there part time as a student in 1904–05 and joined the office force as an engineer after his graduation in September. He remained there until the following spring when the West beckoned.

MONTANA

In May of 1906, he left family and friends to take the Northern Pacific to Butte, Montana, which at that time was the copper mining capital of the world. He visited the smelter at nearby Anaconda, whose immense smoke stack was belching forth the poisonous fumes that were to decimate the beautiful Rocky Mountain foliage for miles around. Fortunately for his health and longevity he was not hired there. He found employment at the Copper Queen Mine located in the mountains outside Sunfield, Montana. He traveled by rail to Red Rock and took the stagecoach from there to Sunfield. Soon after his arrival Papa looked very western in cowboy garb, complete with holstered revolver.

Papa worked for short times in mines or smelters in Montana, Wisconsin, Ontario, Nevada, California, and Minnesota during his early twenties. According to the photo albums, he usually returned to Duluth around the holiday season before traveling to another area early each year. He often found time to return to Houghton, Michigan, to visit Jane Pryor and other friends from his college period.

TREK TO HUDSON BAY

The stories Papa told me of his adventures during this period made a strong impression on me. From March to August 1907, he worked in Cobalt, Ontario for Campbell & Deyell, a mining engineering firm. Photos show work at the Silver Queen and Jacobs mines and many excursions and picnics on Lake Timiscaming and Lake Temagami. While in Cobalt he joined a group of young mining men who set out on an overland prospecting trek from Cochrane, Ontario, to the southernmost part of Hudson Bay, some 150 miles north-northeast.

Their efforts were not successful. They spent several weeks of surveying, working their way through underbrush, sloshing through swamps, and fighting swarms of mosquitoes and black flies. Finally, the party turned back about fifty miles short of its goal. They had made no significant mineral discoveries. Nevertheless, it thrilled me as a child to learn that my father had taken part in such a venture.

NEVADA

In the fall of that same year my father headed west again, this time to Nevada. Southern Nevada was then the scene of another silver and gold rush that had begun at Tonopah at the turn of the century and rivaled the famous Comstock–Big Bonanza rush forty years earlier.

From Reno he took the recently-built Tonopah and Goldfield Railroad (which I was to ride many years later) south to its terminus in Goldfield, then Nevada's most populous city. All of its 20,000 inhabitants had arrived since the discovery of gold there at Rabbit Springs five years earlier. Papa's photos show a sprawling metropolis with several multistoried hotels, a great number of saloons, stores, and other public buildings in the center of a grid of houses, shacks, and tents. The housing shortage was illustrated by his pictures of what he termed dugouts, living areas dug into the side of earthen banks. Again he cut a western figure with his flat-brimmed Stetson, high laced mining boots, open shirt, and gun belt with holstered revolver.

I am not sure why he wore the gun; most historians agree that Goldfield was far more lawful and controlled than earlier mining towns. Many questioned the need for the US troops his photos show arriving in Goldfield in December 1907. Governor Sparks had responded to threats of labor violence by requesting the federal troops. Since 1906, Goldfield had been the scene of many fierce strikes and labor disputes between the mine owners and two big unions: the Wobblies (Industrial Workers of the World) and the Western Federation of Miners. At issue were wages, the mandatory use of company script, and changing rooms. The owners had set up these rooms in an attempt to stem the practice of "high grading" (the removal of valuable ore by hiding it in clothing).

Papa in Goldfield, Nevada in 1907.

About this time word spread throughout southern Nevada that gold-bearing ledges with unbelievably high gold content had been discovered at Hart, California. The strike lay a few miles west of Searchlight, Nevada, scene of a gold rush ten years earlier. Papa went by stage to the Hart area and became a part of some 300 tent dwellers who formed the nucleus of a new boom town. Wagons hauled ore to Searchlight for processing. Entrepreneurs hauled in water and sold it for $8 a barrel. A first class hotel and post office were built

*This photo taken at the stagecoach station in Seachlight, Nevada
shows Grandfather Church seated beside the driver of the stage
that brought him to visit my father in January 1908.*

and law and order established and maintained. A weekly newspaper was started. Although he arrived within a few weeks of the initial discovery, my dad apparently failed to profit from the strike. A few months later the boom was over.

In April he moved north to Rhyolite, Nevada, near Death Valley. The boom town had grown to 6,000 in the three years since prospectors struck gold there in the Bullfrog Hills. The modern town boasted a telephone exchange, hotels, the usual multitude of saloons, and even an opera house, all of which came into existence before the area's highly touted mines began production. The financial panic of 1907 had severely diminished the capital of the large mining companies that had come to exploit the find. Nevertheless, Tramp Consolidated Mining hired Papa. He worked for several months as mining engineer on the tunnels being driven into Bonanza Mountain to remove ore. It was not all work. He still found time for picnics and other socializing with newfound friends.

This period of my father's life is of special interest to me. I had a chance to visit Goldfield and Rhyolite with Papa in 1945 when I was training with a B–24 crew at Tonopah. Dad drove up and spent a weekend showing me what we could find of his old haunts. We saw how these cities, that only thirty-eight years earlier had thousands of inhabitants, had virtually disappeared from the Nevada landscape.

Goldfield was still there with a few buildings, including the four-story Goldfield Hotel, still standing. Since I was below legal drinking age at the time, I told Dad only that several of the married members of our crew had families living at the hotel. I failed to mention earlier visits to its immense and ornate bar on several drunken occasions. Most of the rest of Goldfield no longer existed. It had been devastated by flood in 1913, a massive fire in 1923 that destroyed fifty square blocks, and the ravages of time, weather, and vandals.

Accompanied by three attractive young women, my father and another man set out fromRhyolite for an excursion to the Tramp ranch in Indian Springs, Nevada, 1908.

My father and I survey a desolate scene at Rhyolite, Nevada in 1945.

At Rhyolite there was even less evidence of the boom years. A few remaining shacks set in the barren and windswept Amargosa Desert echoed the feeling of desolation of nearby Death Valley. Apart from a few abandoned mine tunnels and building foundations, the only feature that my dad recognized was Rhyolite's most famous house. It had been reconstructed for use in a Zane Grey movie in the 1920s. It was built of one of the earlier gold rush's most plentiful building materials, discarded liquor bottles.

WITH THE CHIPPEWAS

By late summer of 1908, my father had left the mining camps of Nevada to return to western Minnesota. He went to work for the Northland Pine Company as head of a surveying crew prospecting for minerals. They were mapping the area that included the lakes and streams that form the headwaters of the Mississippi. Much of their work was in and around the White Earth Indian Reservation. During the year-long project Dad got to know a number of the Chippewas who lived in this large reservation. They were friendly and let the surveying crews visit their ceremonies and living areas. Only twelve years before, at nearby Cass Lake, these same Chippewas had fought the US Army. It was the last Indian battle in the US in which Army officers and enlisted men were killed and wounded. Indian friends presented to my father beaded deerskin moccasins and gloves along with an elaborately beaded tobacco pouch. I recently learned that this pouch was appropriated and used by my daughter Sally as a wall decoration during the Flower Days of the 1960s. It is still in her possession.

Above: Chippewa encampment at White Earth Indian Reservation, Minnesota, 1908.

At left: Jane Pryor wears the Chippewa ceremonial pouch presented to my father, 1908.

WHITE SULFUR SPRINGS

In late 1909, Papa traveled back to Montana. Except for a few months in the southeastern corner of the state, he spent most of the next five years in or near White Sulfur Springs, located fifty miles west of Montana's capital city, Helena. There he met John North Ringling, who had become famous along with his six brothers for developing the largest circus organization in the world. Ringling had acquired a great deal of cattle land in the Smith River area north of White Sulfur Springs. He wanted an easier means of getting his cattle to market. He decided to build a railroad from White Sulfur Springs to the Chicago, Milwaukee & St. Paul main line about 25 miles to the south. He hired my dad to help survey the route and plan the grades, bridges, etc. Ringling named the new line the White Sulfur Springs & Yellowstone Park Railroad.

Papa surveyed the route, designed, and supervised the 1909 construction of John Ringling's new rail line that brought rail service to White Sulfur Springs, Montana.

Because the route selected ran through relatively level country, the new line was completed quickly. The first rail shipment of cattle from White Sulfur occurred in November 1910. John Ringling's private Pullman car, "Wisconsin," appeared on a local siding and a big celebration commemorated the town's new status as a rail terminus. Later, when he became county engineer and assayer, Papa operated out of the Smith River Development Company's office on the main street of White Sulfur Springs.

Important to this narrative is the fact that White Sulfur Springs was only sixty miles from the Melville area where the Van Cleves lived. Mutual friends in Helena introduced the 26-year-old bachelor to the Van Cleves. He soon found himself invited to events at the Home Ranch, Hunter Hot Springs, and Crag Eyrie. Most of the parties were at Crag Eyrie, where the recently-married Blakemans (Mother and her husband Tom) threw some grand all-night costume parties that my dad attended.

Mining-related and other engineering assignments in the area around White Sulfur Springs and Helena occupied most of my dad's time during the next few years. He led an active social life in Helena, White Sulfur Springs, and Sweet Grass County. Like his father before him he became active in the Masonic Order. Photos attest to more picnics, fishing trips, and outings often featuring attractive women. It appears that the beautiful Jane Pryor was no longer the focus of his attention. Although he made occasional trips to Wrenshall, Minnesota, to his father's new farm and to Houghton, Michigan, for college reunions, there were no more pictures of Jane.

REVOLUTIONARY MEXICO

Through a Michigan College of Mines classmate, he became superintendent of the San Toy Mine in Chihuahua, Mexico, in the fall of 1914. Mexico had been in the throes of revolution for four years since Porfinio Diaz, its harsh dictator and president for thirty years, had been deposed by revolutionary forces. Chihuahua figured prominently in many of the battles. I have a copy of the safe conduct letter for San Toy representatives under which Papa traveled to Chihuahua. As provisional military governor of Chihuahua, Francisco (Pancho) Villa had signed it.

There was considerable political and military turmoil in the months preceding my father's arrival. President Madera, who succeeded Diaz, was in turn overthrown in a coupe engineered by General Huerta. Other revolutionary leaders, Zapata, Villa, Orozco, and Carranza, continued to battle not only Huerta's new Federalist troops but also among themselves. In the spring of 1914, the US Government that had abetted Huerta's coupe, repudiated Huerta because of the adverse effect the brutal warfare was having on American oil and mining ventures. After a dispute between US Navy officers and Huerta's Federalists, the US Marines occupied the port city of Vera Cruz.

In June of 1914, rebel forces closed on Mexico City—Villa from the north, Obregon from the northwest, and Zapata from the southwest. In July, Huerta fled the country on a German naval vessel. Carranza considered himself the logical choice to succeed Huerta as president but found that the other rebel leaders who were occupying the capitol had different ideas.

As my father entered Mexico at Juarez in October of 1914, a convention of the various rebel factions was taking place in Aguascalientes, 300 miles northwest of Mexico City. After the convention, while my father was work-

My father took this picture of Villa's troops preparing to leave Chihahua City in the fall of 1914.

ing at the San Toy mines outside Chihuahua City, open warfare broke out between these various factions.

In January of 1915, Carranza issued a provisional decree that restored *ejidos*, (lands granted to villages for the use of peons), the constitutional principle that Diaz had abrogated. This first constructive act of the revolution solidified revolutionary support of Carranza and won him diplomatic recognition by the US and Latin American countries as de facto president of Mexico.

Villa, however, continued to battle Carranza forces. His army suffered a major defeat by Obregon forces at Celaya in April of 1915, and he returned to the Durango Mountains south of Chihuahua. Angered at Washington's recognition of Carranza, Villa turned against the American mining interests that he had protected. My mother had told me that my father once missed a train from which several Americans were removed and killed by

Villa forces. By June of 1915, the situation for Americans at San Toy had become too hazardous to continue the mining operations and my father returned to the US. Villa massacred 18 American miners at Santa Isabel in Sonora six months later.

During the balance of 1915, Papa traveled throughout the West and Midwest. He visited Seattle in July for the Shriner's Convention as part of the Helena, Montana contingent. August of 1915, found him in Sweet Grass County at the Blakeman's enjoying one of their all-night parties. Later that month he visited his parents' home in Wrenshall, Minnesota and Mackinac Island, Michigan. In September he traveled on the steamer *Northern Pacific* from Portland, Oregon to San Francisco. Papa spent several

This street scene of Brewery Gulch in Bisbee, Arizona, was photographed by my father in 1916.

days visiting the world's fair that celebrated the city's reconstruction and rebirth after the disastrous 1906 earthquake and fire. He appears to have spent the next few months in California. Albums show him in San Diego in December, where another fair was in progress.

On Christmas Day he was back in Mexico. Intriguing photos at the border town of Naco show him and an attractive woman on top of a train with their luggage. This Sonora town is a few miles from Bisbee, Arizona, where Papa spent the next six months in the engineering department of the Copper Queen Mine. Bisbee was a sprawling boom town complete with streetcars, office buildings, and extensive mining activities.

As he traveled back to Montana from Bisbee in June, he passed through El Paso. There he photographed the tents of some of the large military force Pershing led on an ineffectual punitive expedition into Mexico. They were in pursuit of Villa who had followed up his massacre at Santa Isabel with a raid on Columbus, New Mexico, in which seventeen Americans died.

CAPTAIN CHURCH

Upon his return to Montana, he worked as mining engineer for the Comet Mine at Comet, Montana. While there, he applied for a reserve commission in the army. He expected that the US would be drawn into the expanding war in Europe. After the US declared war on Germany in April 1917, he was ordered to report to army headquarters in nearby Yellowstone Park for Army Officers Reserve Corps examinations.

Papa was very proud of his army service. He went on active duty in September as a captain in the army engineers. After training at Fort Leavenworth, Kansas, he transferred to the 308th Engineers at Camp Sherman, Chillicothe, Ohio. He spent a cold and snowy winter continuing the pontoon bridge training begun at Fort Leavenworth. He was appointed assistant engineering officer of his division. In June 1918, he transferred to Washington Barracks, DC, and took command of the 466th Engineers, a pontoon train unit. He and his unit spent the summer in nearby Maryland testing the practicality of substituting gasoline fueled tractors for the mule power that had moved army pontoon bridge building equipment up to that time. From the looks of the bogged down tractors that Papa photographed, the mules won.

Captain John L. Church at Washington Barracks, DC. 1918

I believe my father married while at Wahington Barracks. There are no pictures or other notations I can find in any of the albums or scrapbooks of either the bride or the event. I knew nothing of this marriage as a child and had assumed my father was a bachelor before marrying my mother. When Mother was telling me of their plans to divorce in 1942, she mentioned that Papa had an earlier marriage. I think she wanted me to see her previous divorce in a better light. I never discussed the matter with either of my parents again. Only when reviewing some of the army documents concerning my father's transfer overseas did I find reference to Mrs. F. Jean Church, wife. Her address was 4200 New Hampshire Avenue NW, Washington, DC. I surmise that this was a "GI insurance marriage" to provide death benefits to a recent acquaintance. I guess the marriage was annulled. In any case, I have no information as to what happened to Jean.

The July 15, 1918 edition of the *Helena Record Herald* carried an article headlined "Would Bridge German Rhine" based on a letter Papa sent from Washington Barracks to one of his Helena friends. I recall seeing this article in one of Grandfather Church's scrapbooks as a youngster. Some of the memorable excerpts that made an impression on me include:

> Captain John L. Church, former resident of Helena and well-known Helena resident, now commanding the 466th Engineers, and stationed at Washington writing to J. Scott Harrison writes, 'My organization is a pontoon section and I am in hopes to bridge the Rhine when we go into Germany...'

> He writes that his command there is an army unit. That means he will not be troubled by majors and colonels, but has for his superior officer a general. The letter states that the talk at Washington about the war is that the next two months will be critical for the allies. If they hold the Germans during that period the war will be as good as won. By next spring, when the Americans get going good in Europe, the German line will begin to be bent back.... He hopes to get over to the other side within two months.

His prediction for his unit's move was accurate. On August 31, 1918, the four officers and 170 enlisted men of the 466th Engineers were ordered to Brooklyn, NY for embarkation. Two days later they were at sea on the *S/S Valari*, bound for Southampton, England. Menus and the shipboard newspaper of the *Valari* attest to the high level amenities that at least the officers received en route.

My grandfather saved the printed safe arrival card all arriving soldiers sent to family members. After a few days in England, Papa's unit crossed

the Channel, arriving in Le Havre September 23. From there they proceeded to Gievres, in the department of Loir et Cher. On October 19, the 466th
moved to the Army Engineers School at Langres in Haute Marne, about 35
miles north of Dijon.

My recent research reveals an interesting tie between the Dijon area, my
father's closest proximity to the Western Front, and Lawrence Clark Powell.
This author studied and wrote in Dijon in the early thirties along with several other young writers from the Pasadena area. Powell's later books,
which chronicle his childhood in South Pasadena, validate my belief that I
was blessed to begin my life in that special area of Southern California.

My father's orders read to report to the commandant of the Bridge
Section "for a course of instruction not to exceed four weeks in pontoon
and heavy timber bridges." Langres was about 75 miles behind the battle
front and about 100 miles from the Rhine River that he had hoped to
bridge. Three weeks after the 466th got to Langres the armistice was signed.
On November 12, General Pershing published General Orders No. 203 to
the American Expeditionary Forces, which stated that the enemy had capit-
ulated and thanked the officers and soldiers who made possible "this glorious result."

One related memory of my Dad comes to mind that may illuminate his
personality and his views on the French. When I was in my thirties I told
my father with some enthusiasm that I had an assignment that would take
me to Paris. He hrrumphed and said he couldn't understand why anyone
would want to go to Paris. "After all," he said, "I was based only about
thirty miles from Paris when I was in France and I never had any desire to
go into the city."

Until I recently completed my perusal of orders, baggage slips, and
other materials in the scrapbooks, I had thought that my father had been in
combat. Now I am not sure. When the 466th demobilized at Camp

Humphries, VA, in January of 1919, the final roster listed 14 men as "losses," but they may not have been combat casualties.

Papa returned to the Helena area after his demobilization. He resumed his mining engineering activities and rejoined his circle of friends, which included the Van Cleve family in Sweet Grass County. The Blakemans were not in Montana. Mother was still in France with the YMCA and her husband Tom was still in the Air Corps. After about a year of working in mines near Helena and Townsend, my dad decided to move to California. That move led to the beginning of these memoirs.

C. Selected Bibliography

Much of the enjoyment I derived from writing these memoirs came from the reading I did to refresh my memory and check the historical and geographic accuracy of my recollections. Some of the books, both nonfiction and fiction, that helped or moved me to put this collection of happenings together are included here. Nonfiction references are listed geographically.

SOUTHERN CALIFORNIA

Apostle, Jane. *South Pasadena: A Centennial History, 1888-1988*. South Pasadena, CA: South Pasadena Public Library, 1987.

Caughey, John and LaRee. *Los Angeles: Biography of a City*. Berkeley: University of California Press, 1976.

Crump, Spencer. *Ride the Big Red Cars*. Los Angeles: Trans Anglo Books, 1962.

Drury, Aubrey. *California: An Intimate Guide*. New York: Harper & Brothers Publishers, 1947.

Haslam, Gerald. *Coming of Age in California: Personal Essays*. Walnut Creek, CA: Devil Mountain Books, 1990.

Henstell, Bruce. *Sunshine and Wealth: Los Angeles in the Twenties and Thirties*. San Francisco: Chronicle Books, 1984.

Houston, James D. *Californians: Searching for the Golden State*. Berkeley: Creative Arts Book Co., 1985.

Long, Raphael F. *Red Car Days: Memories of the Pacific Electric*. Glendale, CA: Interurban Press. 1983.

McWilliams, Carey. *Southern California: An Island on the Land*. Santa Barbara, CA: Peregrine Smith, 1973.

Orcutt, Mary Logan. *Memorabilia of William Warren Orcutt*. Los Angeles: The Fred S. Lang Press, 1945.

Powell, Lawrence Clark. *An Orange Grove Boyhood: Growing Up in Southern California 1910-1928*. Santa Barbara, CA: Capra Press, 1988.

Powell, Lawrence Clark. *Fortune and Friendship: An Autobiography by Lawrence Clark Powell*. NYC: R. R. Bowker Company, 1968.

Powell, Lawrence Clark. *Life Goes On: Twenty More Years of Fortune & Friendship*. Metuchen, NJ: Scarecrow Press, 1986.

Scheid, Ann. *Pasadena: Crown of the Valley*. Northridge, CA: Windsor Publications, 1986.

Starr, Kevin. *Inventing the Dream: California Through the Progressive Era*. New York: Oxford University Press, 1985.

Starr, Kevin. *Material Dreams: Southern California Through the 1920's*. New York: Oxford University Press, 1990.

Stremfel, Michael. *Founding Fortunes of Southern California*. Los Angeles: Los Angeles Business Journal and City National Bank, 1989.

Taylor, Frank J. and Welty. Earl M. *Black Bonanza: How an Oil Hunt Grew into the Union Oil Company of California*. New York: Whittlesey House, McGraw-Hill Book Company, Inc., 1950.

Young, Betty Lou. *Our First Century: Los Angeles Athletic Club*. Los Angeles: LAAC Press, 1979.

MONTANA

Connolly, Christopher P. *The Devil Learns to Vote: The Story of Montana*. New York: Covici, Friede, Inc., 1938.

Dawson, Patrick. *Mr. Rodeo: The Big Bronc Years of Leo Cremer*. Livingston, MT: Cayuse Press, 1986.

Doig, Ivan. *Heart Earth: A Memoir*. New York: Penguin Books, 1993.

Doig, Ivan. *This House of Sky: Landscapes of a Western Mind*. New York: A Harvest/HBJ Book, Harcourt Brace Jovanovich, 1980.

Kittredge, William and Smith, Annick, Editors. *The Last Best Place: A Montana Anthology*. Helena: Montana Historical Society Press, 1988

Mockel, Myrtle. *Dusty Corrals*. Billings: Western Printing & Lithography, 1972.

Van Cleve, Spike. *40 Years' Gatherin's*. Kansas City, MO: The Lowell Press, 1977.

Van Cleve, Spike. *A Day Late and A Dollar Short*. Kansas City, MO: The Lowell Press, 1982.

THE WEST IN GENERAL

Backes, Clarus. *Growing Up Western: Recollections by Dee Brown, A.B. Guthrie, Jr., David Lavender, Wright Morris, Clyde Rice, Wallace Stegner, Frank Waters*. New York: Alfred A. Knopf, 1990.

Black, Naomi. *Dude Ranches of the American West*. Lexington, MA: The Stephen Greene Press, 1988.

DeVoto, Bernard. *The Course of Empire*. Boston: Houghton Mifflin Company, 1952.

Kittredge, William. *Hole in the Sky: A Memoir*. New York: Vintage Books, Random House, 1992.

Paher, Stanley W. *Nevada Ghost Towns & Mining Camps*. Las Vegas: Nevada Publications, 1970.

Reisner, Marc. *Cadillac Desert: The American West and its Disappearing Water*. New York: Viking Penguin, 1986.

Stegner, Wallace. *Where the Bluebird Sings to the Lemonade Springs: Living and Writing in the West*. New York: Random House, 1992.

Stegner, Wallace. *Wolf Willow: A History, a Story, and a Memory of the Last Plains Frontier*. New York: The Viking Press, 1962.

Watkins, T.H., Watkins, Joan, Editors. *The West: A Treasury of Art and Literature*.

New York: Beaux Arts Editions, 1994.

Van Cleve, Charlotte Ouisconsin. *Three Score Years and Ten: Life-long Memories of Fort Snelling, Minnesota and Other Parts of the West*. Minneapolis: Harrison-Smith, 1888.

OTHER

Boyne, Walter J. *Silver Wings: A History of the United States Air Force*. New York: Simon and Schuster, 1993.

Ruiz, Ramon, E. *Triumphs and Tragedy: A History of the Mexican People*. New York: Norton, 1992.

Werstein, Irving. *Land & Liberty, the Mexican Revolution (1910-1919)*. New York: Cowles Book, 1971.

FICTION

Doig, Ivan. *Dancing at the Rascal Fair*. New York: Harper Perennial, Harper Collins Publishers, 1987.

Doig, Ivan. *English Creek*. New York: Harper Collins Publishers, 1984.

Doig, Ivan. *Ride With Me, Mariah Montana*. New York: Penguin Books, 1990.

Guthrie, A.B. Jr. *The Big Sky*. New York: Houghton Mifflin, 1952.

Guthrie, A.B. Jr. *The Way West*. New York: Houghton Mifflin, 1952.

Stegner, Wallace. *Angle of Repose*. New York: Doubleday & Company, 1971

Stegner, Wallace. *The Big Rock Candy Mountain*. New York: Doubleday & Company, 1943.

Acknowledgments

Many people have generously contributed their time and talents to this effort. My daughter, Sally Petersen, has provided continuing aid and encouragement. She has played a major role, from reviewing the earliest manuscripts to final proofing. Lisa Smith has been a superb editor, meticulous, and unrelenting in educating me in matters of style, presentation, and publishing. Rob Roehrick applied his considerable artistic skills to the cover design and its production.

Jim Gradolph has been my computer guru and the principal source of help with the hardware and software involved. Others like David Kline, Dennis Love, Al Ardell, and Scott Stokes have provided computer graphics assistance and advice. At each stage of the project, the needed technical production help just seemed to appear.

My research efforts were greatly abetted by relatives, friends, and an often unsung resource for writers, research librarians. Relatives who provided important information included my niece, Bebe Blakeman Kaarstad, and cousins, Tack Van Cleve and Shelly Carroccia. Many of the characters in these tales contributed information and reviewed versions of the manuscript including Marilyn Wagner Raymond, George Hall, Ben Reinhold, Ralph Wood, Art Krause, Mickey Magee Church, and Ruth Maxwell Buffington.

Some libraries and museums where I worked, and whose staffs were most helpful: the South Pasadena Public Library; the Sutro State Library in San Francisco; the San Francisco City Library; the Marin County Library; the New York City Library; the Montana State University Library in Bozeman; the Park County Museum in Livingston, Montana; the Big Timber Public Library and the Pioneer Museum in Big Timber, Montana; and the Central Nevada Museum in Tonopah, Nevada.

Finally, I am most grateful for the unfailing love, help, and patient support provided by my dear wife Fran.